The Four Powers in Space

America's Soul As of October 18, 2018

by Susan J. Kokinda

These are edited remarks given by Michigan LaRouche PAC coordinator Susan J. Kokinda, on LaRouche PAC's weekly Fireside Chat broadcast of Oct. 18, 2018.

I want to address the subjective side of the political process that is unfolding right now, and I want to start by reading a letter to the editor that was in the Sunday *Detroit Free Press*. It's addressing in particular the Senate campaign, where we have an incumbent Democratic Senator, Debbie Stabenow. This is from somebody in one of the northern suburbs of Detroit. The author writes the following.

Make no mistake. My certain vote for Debbie Stabenow is no longer. One who normally votes for the most qualified candidate, will vote entirely Republican in this coming election.

The despicable, underhanded, unfair, base tactics of the Democrats, gleefully willing to ruin a good man because they have different philosophies and politics, eliminates any Democrats as a voting choice for me.

I cringed when I heard Debbie Stabenow vote no on Judge Brett Kavanaugh's nomination. Well, I also get to vote no in November.

The Democratic talking point that suburban women will now vote Democratic because of this fight is wishful thinking. There is not one, let me repeat that, not one woman I know, Democrat or Republican, who is now going to vote Democratic. *All* plan to vote Republican.

Democrats have completely and finally committed political suicide.

I think there's actually a poetic principle embedded in that letter, whether the writer knows it or not, because I think the attacks on Kavanaugh, and really, the attacks on the Constitution itself that the Democrats carried out in the recent weeks, have sparked a shift in the political process, and it's taking it to a higher level. It's what we call "the mass strike," but more importantly it's a movement which is not about particulars, but rather it's a profound shift to a higher level.

This is different from the intense support which the Trump base has been giving him during his whole Presidency. President Trump has been under unbelievable attack; his base has been very mobilized and very supportive. But this is different. These are new layers of the population which are now outraged at the Democratic Party and the media. And I don't think they necessarily understand what's behind it—as we do—but this is causing a profound shift in the country.

A Poetic Principle of Change

I call this a "poetic principle," because it echoes something which you can find in Aeschylus' *Prometheus Bound*. Those of you who were on the call I did about a month and a half ago, remember that I spoke about that play, which describes the fate of Prometheus, who defended mankind from the Olympian god Zeus, and Zeus, of course, represents the oligarchy. Today, some people call it "the elite" or the "deep state"—we correctly call it the "British Empire." And Prometheus is chained to a rock and he's tortured for what's supposed to be eternity, because he gave mankind the gift of fire and gave him the arts and the sciences which made man, man.

Now the first few times I read this play, there was a part in it which completely puzzled me. The story is going along; Prometheus is describing what has happened to him to his audience. His audience includes Hermes, the messenger god, whose basic role is to tell Prometheus he ought to make a plea bargain with Zeus.

But then he has a Chorus of sea nymphs, who are very sympathetic, but they sort of have the attitude of "Really? What did you expect? You took on Zeus; you should have expected something like this to happen." So, there's a kind of resignation and fear over the power and the cruelty of Zeus and the Olympian gods.

But then you get to the part of the play which I didn't understand for a while. A cow shows up, a frenzied, maddened cow shows up, being stung by gadflies. And it turns out this is actually a young maiden, Io, who had been raped by Zeus, and then, because Zeus's wife was jealous, she turned this young woman into a cow to be stung by gadflies, and this poor woman/cow has fled from Greece to the Caucasus, where Prometheus is, and she tells her story to Prometheus and the Chorus. And suddenly, the Chorus *changes*.

This living image of the cruelty of Zeus and the Olympians—not just against someone who has defied them, like Prometheus did, and as LaRouche has always done, and as Trump is doing—but against this maiden, treating her like an animal (and actually turning her into an animal), that changes the Chorus. They decide to stand with Prometheus. They move beyond their fear of the oligarchy and they join with Prometheus as he continues to defy Zeus. And it represents a very dramatic shift in the whole direction of this play.

A Principled Shift in Thinking

And I think what you're seeing in that letter to the editor, is that same thing is happening, a principle of justice is suddenly awakened in the American population. I don't know if the writer likes Judge Kavanaugh's judicial philosophy. He may not like many or most of Trump's policies. He may not even like some of the Republicans for whom he's voting. But it's a reflection of the fact that this has gone beyond the domain of issues, into a different domain, and this is what is called the "mass strike," where the population is moved by higher principles, not the laundry list of "issues." Instead, it's responding to something else.

The issues are still there. If you turn on the TV and watch any campaign ads, with few exceptions, it's mostly the attack politics, the laundry list of issues. But if this midterm is fought over issues like immigration or health care, I'm not so certain of the outcome. Instead, it has to be transformed, as I think we're seeing it being transformed. Here especially in the Midwest, this is what we set out to do on Aug. 16, when we issued our national campaign statement on the countdown to the consequential midterm elections. We wanted to make clear to people that the midterm elections were a fight between two paradigms, whether we can go forward, with Trump into a new paradigm of peace and economic cooperation, or whether we're going to be dragged back into the war and economic disintegration policies.

As I'm sure, as most people on this call know, what we laid out in that statement is three standards which people should hold their candidates to—those three standards being: (1) Stopping the attacks on the President and going after the perpetrators of these attacks, (2) Supporting working with Russia and China, as President Trump clearly wan ts to do, and (3) most fundamentally, the full body of LaRouche's policies, which will free the nation from Wall Street, and launch a science-driven economic policy, in collaboration with Russia, China, India and the other great powers.

We can see the effect of our intervention, I think especially in the Midwest, because we've triggered something and we're tapping into something which is of this higher character. We're seeing it when we intervene in Trump rallies and go to political events, and in the form of some of these campaigns that Dennis [Speed] referenced, which I'll get to in a minute. I want to give you an example of the quality of response we're getting.

Last week, as people may know, President Trump held a series of rallies in the Midwest. We were able to send a team of two people down to the one in southern Ohio, near Cincinnati, and then the second one, the next day, was about 100 miles away in Kentucky. Between those two rallies, we distributed about 4,000 copies of our midterm elections strategy leaflet. We got over 200 contacts, of people who gave us either their emails or their phone numbers to be in touch, and we were challenging people to set the agenda on these three defining questions.

Obviously, on the first pledge, defending the President—well, people were there to defend the President; they were standing in the cold for six hours or so, or more, in order to be able to get in to see him. And of course, people were telling us, "I defend the President, I'm going to vote Republican, all my friends are going to vote Republican"; and we were saying to them, that's not why we're here.

We're here because you have to take this leaflet, and you have to go out, and you have to recruit blue collar workers, and Democrats and Independents, and they have to be ready for the next big fight, because President Trump is going to have to take on Wall Street and the City of London, because this financial system is going to come down. And the question is: Is it going to come down on our terms, or is it going to come down on the enemy's terms?

We were telling them, the President *does have* the international relationships to do this. He's got the relationship with Xi Jinping and Putin, and to a certain degree, India's Prime Minister Narendra Modi. But he's going to need a movement that actually will back him up and understands what the fight is all about.

A Sober but Optimistic Response

We got a quite interesting response from people, a very sober but optimistic response that this is the fight that we have to be ready for, and that we do have to recruit broader layers. This was different from some of the previous rallies we'd gone to; we went to the one down in Columbus in July and then, earlier in April, when Trump was here in Michigan. In those earlier events, we were largely eliciting a very strong response on the question of the British, because it was new to people, but they knew that they needed to understand what we were saying. Now, individuals such as Joe diGenova and George Papadopoulos, and others, have put that out there, and it's something which is in people's frame of reference in terms of how they're waging this fight.

In the most recent events, what has become clear is the people are ready for profound ideas. To give you a sense of some of the responses, obviously, you're talking about Ohio, where LaRouche has had a presence for decades and decades—one guy wearing his Teamster jacket came up and said. "LaRouche? Isn't he a communist?" And then he burst out laughing and he said, "Gimme a bunch of those leaflets!" We were getting a very strong indication that people are ready to organize, as this guy represented. One person said, "Give me a bunch of those leaflets. I have to take 'em to work." And we said, "Yeah? Where do you work?" He said, "I'm a state legislator; I'm going to take them to the state capitol." People were remembering LaRouche's role in the Strategic Defense Initiative, and so on.

People are ready for the bigger ideas, and really, the bigger fight. We were also saying, it's obvious that the Democratic Party is not going to hold its base, with what they did to Kavanaugh, with the identity politics and mob violence, and people can see that—that the Democratic Party, as that writer said, has committed its final "political suicide."

Beyond Party Labels

But we're not just seeing a rejection of the Democratic Party. We have a unique candidate running for U.S. Senate here in the state of Michigan. We have saturated the political environment here with our campaign strategy statement, and it's reflected in the way that John James, the Republican candidate for U.S. Senate running against Debbie Stabenow, is conducting his campaign. James is young, a 38-year-old; he's a West Point graduate; he was a combat pilot in Iraq; he's African American, he runs his family's business. He won the Republican primary with the backing of Trump, who came in, pretty much at the last minute, and helped him defeat a very standard, monetarist Republican businessman.

He does have the Republican nomination, but he is unabashedly running as a *de facto* Independent. He never misses an occasion to attack both political parties, doing it in his campaign ads, in interviews; he did it in the debate he had with Debbie Stabenow the other day. He is saying, both political parties have failed; all they do is pit us against each other. He says, my message is not Democrat or Republican, my message isn't black or white; he's attacking the policies that have failed the cities, failed the schools, failed the veterans. In fact, he says that when he came back from Iraq, he saw more devastation in Detroit than he saw in the Iraq war.

Some Republicans are nervous about the fact that he says he isn't going to the Senate to represent the Republican Party: He's going to represent all the people of Michigan. And, this obviously is not bothering Donald Trump. Yesterday, Trump put out a tweet, once again praising John James to the sky, calling him a "star," calling on the people of Michigan to recognize what they have and to vote for him.

There was also a rally here for James—Donald Trump, Jr., came in to host the rally. They had to change the venue three times because of the number of people who were responding and sending their RSVP. The first venue was 900 people; then it was 1,500 people, and the fire marshal just kept saying, "Nope, can't do it here"; so, they ended up in a venue which held, I think, 4,000 people. It looks like they actually pulled 4,000 people for this rally yesterday.

Again, we were there organizing the people going in, and as we had seen elsewhere, people were ready to move. What we had seen down in Ohio and Kentucky, we saw again here, including trade unionists coming out in open support. We talked to a guy from the United Auto Workers (UAW) who was there, and he said, Look, there's a lot of people in the UAW who support Trump. They're not going to say it publicly, but that support is there.

At the same time, our role is being increasingly acknowledged. We spoke to a high-level GOP representative from the state whom we had met a couple of weeks earlier and had an extensive discussion on the looming financial crisis. And this person thanked us profusely for what we're doing with our intervention into these midterm elections.

John James is running a campaign parallel to ours in a certain sense. But we also have a Republican congressional candidate, who is more than parallel. He has openly embraced the LaRouche program. His name is Jeff Jones (and I know, it's easy to get John James and Jeff Jones confused), but Jeff is running in one of these Detroit suburb areas as a Republican. He's a real long shot, whereas John James is rapidly closing the gap with Debbie Stabenow and could pull off the upset of the 2018 election. But the congressional candidate, Jeff Jones, like the Senate candidate, is attacking the failure of policy over the last 50 years, not just talking about Barack Obama and the last eight years. He's talking about the fact that there has been a profound failure in the nation for a half-century.

Now, there's one other reflection I want to mention in terms of this independent shift. It was reported out of our office in Baltimore, that the board of elections in Maryland, which people probably know is very Democratic, very blue—the board of elections is reporting that the overwhelming number of new registrations to vote are coming in as Independents, not as Democrats and not as Republicans.

The Mandate of Heaven

And this is exactly what LaRouche forecast on his 90th birthday, six years ago in 2012. He called for the end of the two-party system, and called for freeing the nation from the death grip of these partisan politics, such that we can actually conduct policy—as a republic is supposed to—and this is what I think we're seeing unfold.

Before I end, I want to take it out of the domain of politics and put people up on the stage of history, by referencing a remarkable piece that Lyndon LaRouche wrote from his jail cell, in 1989. And remember, he was put in that jail cell, courtesy of the Get LaRouche Task Force, which was launched by Robert Mueller's indictment a couple of years earlier. This document that LaRouche wrote was entitled, "The Great Crisis of 1989-1992," and he wrote it in July, prior to the fall of the Berlin Wall. But Lyndon LaRouche is Promethean, he has foresight, and he saw it coming, and he wrote of the worldwide revolutions. He said,

Every true revolutionary upsurge in history is distinguished by two general preconditions. First, it must become widely sensed that the existing regime has lost the Mandate of Heaven. Visibly, the signs are that God has turned his face against that regime.

The "Mandate of Heaven," as some people may know, is a concept from ancient Chinese culture; it's a Confucian concept, that there are universal principles, and if a government or a ruler violates those universal principles then it will lose the Mandate of Heaven and its regime will fall. Clearly, this is what is now happening to the British Empire and its policies, and its minions in the Democratic Party and the Bush/Cheney wing of the Republican Party, as well as all of the governments and parties in Western Europe, which we're watching fail spectacularly at this point. There is this rejection of those institutions which have lost the Mandate of Heaven.

This is why LaRouche characterized Trump's election in 2016 as part of a movement of international change. I think that part is clear—the loss of the mandate. We see it on the streets, we see it in letters to the editor. But then, Mr. LaRouche says, there's a second precondition to a revolutionary upsurge. And he says, "The new government implicit in a revolutionary movement, must be seen as qualified to receive the Mandate of Heaven."

That is where we come in. It's not enough to just reject globalization or Wall Street, or identity politics, or manmade climate change, or liberals or Democrats. We have to be prepared to define the qualified policies in order to receive the Mandate of Heaven. Mr. La-Rouche identifies what the most essential role of government in that regard is, and he says it is to "shape the entire nation's relationship to the physical universe." Most people don't think about government in those terms, but that, of course, is the essence of LaRouche's economic policy—to define the principles of economics that will shape a nation's successful relationship to the physical universe.

Today, twenty years after LaRouche wrote that paper, we can see that governments that have successfully done that—like China with its New Silk Road policy—are in essence leading the world into a new paradigm. That is the real challenge that lies beyond the midterm elections. I'll conclude with the fact that our experience in organizing in the Midwest—seeing how some of these Independent candidates are beginning to emerge—proves that the population really is ready for that challenge.

EIR**Contents**

www.larouchepub.com Volume 45, Number 43, October 26, 2018

Cover This Week

The International Space Station, in a photo taken from the Space Shuttle after undocking, 2010.

NASA

THE FOUR POWERS IN SPACE

Moon-Mars Crash Program Under a Four-Power Agreement

by Michael James Carr

Oct. 21—Gigantic forces are in motion under the surface of today's events. The Anglo-Dutch imperial system which runs today's world from the City of London and its subsidiary of Wall Street, will never give up. They will fight every inch of the way. But nevertheless, there is such a constellation of forces today— as reflected in the current leadership of the United States, China, Russia and India—that over the coming weeks and months, these Four Powers can join together to discuss, to negotiate, and then to create, a new world credit system. This will be a New Bretton Woods system as Lyndon LaRouche designed it, which can end monetarism and the millennia-old system of empire forever.

Earthrise photographed from Apollo 8, Christmas Eve 1968.

Not a monetary system, but a fixed-parity credit system. On the national level of perfectly sovereign nation states, and on the international level through agreements between those sovereign states, masses of new, non-inflationary credit will be issued. It will be non-inflationary because it will only be issued for creditworthy productive purposes, never for speculation or overhead, so that the productive use of the credit issued will later pay it back. Interest rates will be under 2%.

The biggest new direction for such international credits will be for high-technology capital exports from nations such as the United States, Japan and Germany, into less-developed countries. Only under a fixed-parity system is such a volume of long-term, low-interest international lending possible. Other major new directions for new credits will be space exploration, as we discuss below, and fusion power.

This is no Utopia, but it will at last permit us to meet the critical tasks of our nations and of humanity, in exactly the the same way that we meet critical objectives in wartime—not in the Bush-Obama "wars of choice," but in real wars for national survival. In such a war, credits are extended to meet necessary objectives without regard to any competing claims, even if it means creating entire new industries from scratch overnight, as Franklin Roosevelt created the aluminum industry overnight, ignoring the screams of Wall Street. We saw something of the same thing in the Project Apollo of John F. Kennedy and his contemporaries who had returned from World War II.

This is a system in which governments (national,

state and local) will be able to build what is necessary to provide for the future: high-speed rail, water systems, electrical power systems, and so on. The government projects and contracts in all of these areas build up a network of contractors and suppliers who can produce what is necessary to complete the government projects. These contractors and suppliers get the same access to credit as the government agencies, to be able to create the productive powers necessary to meet their government contracts.

This process builds up an array of individuals, companies, schools and so on (hereafter we shall just call them entities) with competence in many areas, but most important in the area of solving problems. Their real-world physical activity is the primary source of progress in physical science and technology. Computer modeling is no substitute for building and testing.

It is beyond the scope of this article to go through it in all detail, but just think about how the progression works: Andrew Carnegie, who first worked for a railroad, took up steel fabrication to build a railroad bridge across the Mississippi, and basically built the modern steel industry. Thomas Edison, who worked for telegraph companies, later created the electric power industry and made modern telephony possible with a viable microphone. Henry Ford, who worked for Edison, later created the modern automotive industry. William Shockley, who worked for AT&T's Bell Labs, in attempting to create mass-produced transistors, hired Robert Noyce who came up with integrated circuits and then central processing units. These are just a few examples from American history.

The basic idea here is that in a credit system, any competent entity with an idea of how to solve a necessary problem, and with a degree of rigorous determination, can get the credit to build it. This is why places such as Detroit and Houston are dotted with small and medium-sized plants which produce all sorts of specialized equipment relating to the automotive and general manufacturing industries, or, in the case of Houston, to the petrochemical and space industries.

Further, when coupled with a fair trade (not free trade) policy, it means that every country of any significant population begins to build up a "full set economy"—an economy which has capabilities to produce most of its needs in most areas domestically, and, most important, prototypes of completely new production processes. No longer are the imperial middlemen allowed to create artificial surpluses or shortages or artificial swings in currency values, in order to force nations into submission. Nations become *actually independent* and sovereign. Citizens become productive, independent and *creative*. So, it will be in this developing environment in which we will be building the global cooperation necessary to colonize the Moon and Mars.

Under national banking and fixed exchange rates, even the smallest and previously poorest of nations will eventually be able to put Lyndon LaRouche's prescribed minimum of 5% of GDP into Research & Development (R&D). In that case, the global efforts at space R&D become the organizing principle around which every area of research revolves. Every problem encountered by Mankind in settling the Moon and Mars is also faced in some degree here on Earth. If we can solve a problem for space travel, we can solve its analogue on Earth. Nearly every earthbound problem could be considered a subset of the problems faced in space.

In that light, space science and space engineering become the organizing principle around which civilization better organizes itself! Imagine, for example, populating the Sahara Desert or far North Siberia. If successful settlements can be built on the Moon and Mars, then they can be built in the "wastelands" of Earth. It is merely a matter of controlling the environment—instead of the submission of Man to the whims of the environment which the British Empire demands.

NASA's Special Role

But the organizing principle requires physical embodiment. It requires a Sergei Korolyov, a Wernher von Braun, or a Qian Xuesen. Such people are alive today (indeed in greater numbers), but they have not been given adequate backup. Once we restore a Hamiltonian credit system to the United States and establish national banking as an international norm of state sovereignty, then scientific and engineering leadership will be allowed to function again. Putting bold ideas into physical form, and running them through rigorous testing and evaluation, will not only be permitted, but promoted.

We applaud, honor and promote the rapid progress being made by China, India, and the newly emerging space programs of the world, but NASA has a special

An artist's conception of Lyndon LaRouche's vision of a city on Mars.

leadership role to play in enabling the global space program to function at its optimum.

As America is a "nation of nations," it is looked to by others to play a special role of combining the best from each nation and each culture, to put together a brighter future for all of us. And NASA's history of achievement gives it a special stature.

When President Trump and NASA put forward a general plan along the lines we will lay out here— backed up by a revived Hamiltonian credit system—to settle and develop the Moon and Mars, every national government, every university, every company, and every student with an interest in this project will be happy to coordinate activity with NASA. The building and administration of the International Space Station (ISS)—via cooperation among 15 nations along with many companies and universities—is a model for the Moon-Mars project.

For future success, this model must become universal. NASA will not dictate, but will simply lay out the overall plan, and identify the problems to be solved and the types of hardware to be created. Each participant will volunteer to accept an area of responsibility and outline a plan to fulfill it. NASA will play a coordinat-

ing and integrating role, while also accepting important responsibilities itself in areas critical for the project, and effectively acting as guarantor of ultimate success overall.

Russia's space agency Roscosmos, for example, would likely offer to further develop its space nuclear power systems among other areas. Canada's Canadian Space Agency (CSA) might offer to take up the design and building of space construction equipment, after its experience in creating robotic arms for the ISS and Space Shuttle. China, after its incredible success in growing plants in arid desert sand, might take on the project of growing plants in the lunar and martian regoliths. Private corporations like SpaceX, with some demonstrated competencies but also somewhat fanciful ideas about Mars colonization, will also be brought in to play an important role in a competently designed and managed plan. Enthusiasm is a necessity, but must always be partnered with rigor.

This project is so big, so complex, and so daunting, that there will be enough work to keep all of humanity's researchers, dreamers, engineers, architects and manufacturers busy for a long time to come. As in a choral symphony, each will be able to take pride in accomplishing an important part of the overall project. And, it will serve to uplift Mankind's vision while spreading prosperity across the globe and beyond.

Once the decision is taken to act, everything changes.

No longer will investigators be forced to sacrifice viable programs to keep others alive, sacrificing a left arm in order to preserve a right arm. Researchers, stuck in the labs and universities with ideas and plans but no resources, will suddenly get the resources to solve the problems facing space development.

Immediately, the ongoing regime of active cooperation and sharing of resources in the current robotic exploration of Mars, for example, will be greatly expanded. Yet the risks and demands of human exploration

There will be no more cases like that of the X-38 International Space Station (ISS) Crew Return Vehicle: 90% built, but canceled because of the lack of money to test it in orbit. Here is the NASA Johnson Space Center team which built the X-38, pictured at the closing of the program. Shown left and right are two 80%-scale drop-test vehicles, and at rear the 90% built orbital test vehicle. The Crew Return Vehicle would have been able to safely glide an entire ISS crew of seven back to Earth from an emergency aboard the ISS.

regulations, and general hysteria run by the FBI and the media, to prevent the natural cooperation of China with the United States in space. This is not a recent phenomenon, nor is President Trump the only victim. The founder of the Chinese nuclear and space programs was Qian Xuesen (Tsien Hsue-shen), a Hangzhou, China-born Caltech professor, who was one of the three founders of NASA's Jet Propulsion Laboratory. Qian had sought American citizenship, but he was driven out of the United States and back to China in 1955, in the British-instigated, anti-communist hysteria of that period. He had not been permitted to continue building the space program in America, so he had to found one back in China.

One little-known fact about China will help to clarify China's intentions toward Americans. Today, every schoolchild in China, starting in kindergarten, is required to learn the American English language, in addition to Mandarin. There are nearly as many students of English in China, about 300 million, as there are Americans altogether. China is making great efforts to be able to better integrate into playing an important role in the world of scientific

and colonization are so enormously greater, that success in these manned missions will demand a far more integrated effort.

The October 11, 2018 "successful failure" of a Roscosmos manned rocket launch to the ISS, and NASA's response to it, have demonstrated once again the determination of the participating national space agencies to resolutely cooperate and support each other. The lessons learned in the ISS project will form the basis upon which to build a successful Moon base that becomes a Moon settlement—Krafft Ehricke's Selenopolis. The Moon experience will become the basis upon which to expand outward to Mars colonization.

A Short Digression

We digress here for a moment to note that an important aspect of the Four-Power agreement overthrowing British world domination, will be the repeal of the British-instigated laws,

A painting by visionary space pioneer Krafft Ehricke of the interior of the lunar city Selenopolis at Christmas.

and technological progress. If we finally shut down the British/FBI witch hunt apparatus, we should expect the China National Space Agency (CNSA) to assume its natural role, and not only participate in the project, but take up important responsibilities within it.

Because of the long-developed relationship of mutual trust, respect and friendship going back to the time of the Apollo-Soyuz Test Project of 1975, British-FBI operations against Russian-American cooperation in space have not been able to be as effective as those against China. And, any astronaut will tell you that NASA would never have accomplished what it has, had it not been spurred on by the successes of the Russian space program.

The Wolf Amendment of 2011, which prohibits co-operation between NASA and CNSA, has shut down most routine communications across the Pacific. It is high time to clear out the old land-mines left behind by the Empire on its way out.

Problems, Problems . . .

Some agencies may put forward variations or alternatives to what we outline here, but the overall requirements of a Moon-Mars program for exploration and colonization were already outlined long ago by Krafft Ehricke, Lyndon LaRouche, and, to a lesser degree, the 1986 National Commission on Space. There have been only a few subsequent technological and political changes which require revisions.

As with the Apollo Project of the 1960s, we are dealing with a critical path of problems to be solved. Each solved problem affects all of the subsequent problems in the path; nevertheless, we don't tackle these problems sequentially, but simultaneously. In this way, as unknowns are resolved, workable architectures begin to appear out of the haze of uncertainty. The problems to be overcome are huge but manageable. Here are some:

- Compact fusion and fission propulsion systems
- Routine spaceplane access to low Earth orbit (LEO) for humans and delicate hardware
- Completely new, heavy-lift maglev launch technology
- Removal or control of LEO space junk
- New construction techniques for lunar and martian settlements
- Technologies to "live off the land" on the Moon and Mars

- Mining and manufacturing technologies
- Technologies for space farming and food preparation
- Air and water recycling and creation
- Healthcare in space
- Space defense against harmful radiation and meteorite impacts
- Psychological effects of long-term separation from Earth
- Physiological and psychological effects of childhood development on the Moon and Mars.

Since about 1967, which saw the peak of Apollo Project funding along with the beginning of the British Tavistock Institute's all-out assault on American scientific progress, the American space program has turned away from pursuing revolutionary "best solution" technologies, towards "cost effective" or "off the shelf" derivative technologies instead. Yet "off the shelf" technologies actually tend to cost more—because they do not lead to revolutionary effects throughout the rest of the economy. For the space program does not return revenue paid out by the Man in the Moon or by little green Martians, but rather through the transformation of the earthly economy by new ideas and technologies transmitted out of the program.

It is this conveyor belt of new technologies and optimism fed into the American economy which led to returns of far more than $10 for each dollar invested into the revolutionary Apollo Project. And, even this is really a faulty measure of value, because the power at the command of one dollar before Apollo was much inferior to the power at the command of a dollar after Apollo had transformed the technologies of every area of product and production.

Having understood this much, it is best practice to put resources into multiple possible solutions for a problem (even into apparently "far out" possible solutions), because the successful revolutionary solution will more than pay for the other failed solutions. And in fact, the economic consequences of such failures can be enormously beneficial.

Columbus failed in his experimental journey to China, yet the failed experiment became the basis for a civilizational transformation, precisely because of its unexpected result. Like Columbus, we may not reach exactly the objectives we project in every initiative; however, it is precisely the unexpected results of an all-out campaign to solve problems which generate new knowledge and thus new powers of humanity as a whole. Those who believe that "we already know it all" have a lot to learn!

With this physical-economic standpoint in mind, we will take a look at NASA's future. We shall maintain and expand current efforts funded at rates consistent with the earliest possible safe deployments of new capabilities for the ISS, the Space Launch System, the Webb Telescope, deep space probes, etc. However, with the new responsibilities NASA will assume, we will make adequate funding available to meet its new obligations.

So, for starters, we shall be speaking about tripling the NASA budget to the range of $50 billion plus, per year. This is a ballpark figure which may see further growth over time as NASA projects move up its "Application Readiness Levels" ladder from research projects into operational hardware.

Similarly, we should expect that especially Russia, China, India, Europe, Japan and Korea—as nations or groupings with leading space capabilities—would also double or triple their commitments to space research. Newly developing space efforts, such as those of South Africa, Nigeria, Brazil and Argentina, would be wise to expand efforts by even greater multiples.

Maintaining Hubble

One of the most important space projects of all time has been the continuing success of the Hubble Space Telescope project. The new Webb Telescope will also provide incredible returns, but it will not be a replacement; the two telescopes operate in different frequency ranges.

Hubble has completely changed Man's perceptions of the Universe. The last Shuttle mission to service it, took place in 2009; we need to re-establish a capability to service it on a timely basis. We need a space truck and we will need it in roughly five years. Here is a case where international cooperation and timing is of the essence: We are talking about building a capability which is mostly based upon known technologies. Much of it could be put together from test articles left over from the Shuttle, Spacelab and ISS projects in Canada,

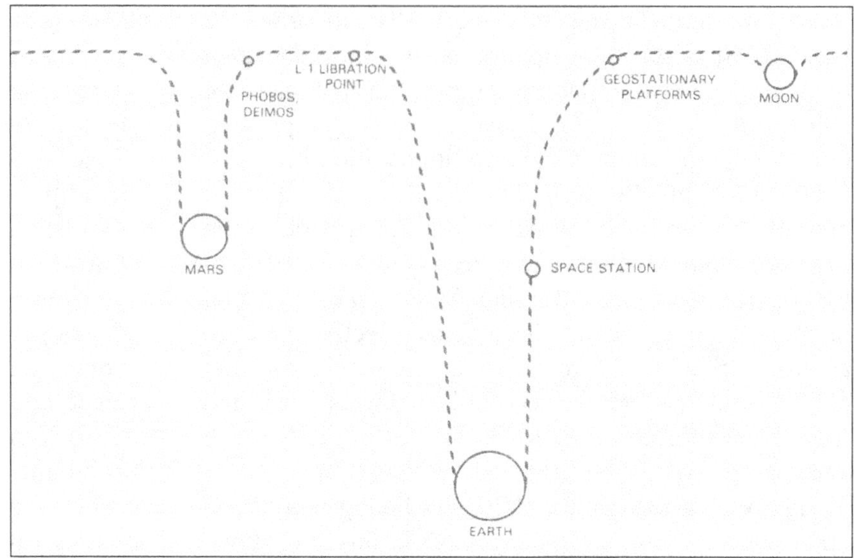

From: *Pioneering The Space Frontier* by the National Commission on Space, 1986

In the "Gravity Well" graphic above you see the relative effort required to reach Low Earth Orbit in the vicinity of the Space Station, as against achieving Geostationary Orbit or the Moon. You also see that the relatively small Gravity Well of the Moon makes it an ideal pit stop to pick up supplies and fuel en route to anywhere else.

Europe and the United States—but this project needs one agency or company to put forward an integrated design. This must be put on a high priority and started now.

What will be required is a spacecraft with some of the capabilities of the Shuttle. However, this new spacecraft will be docked to the ISS and have no need of re-entry capability. It will require a pressurized module for ISS docking, and an airlock to allow astronauts to do spacewalk service work on the Hubble (or other spacecraft in other situations). It will need a sort of flatbed on which to attach parts, and upon which a satellite may be mounted for servicing; and it must feature an arm like the Shuttle's "Canadarm" (the Shuttle Remote Manipulator System, or SRMS).

Most important, it will have to be able to carry a very large propellant supply, in order to navigate between the orbital altitudes and inclinations of the ISS and various satellites, such as the Hubble. It will naturally need to be refueled in orbit (not necessarily while attached to the ISS).

From Earth to Orbit

Turning back now to the longer-term issues, problem number one is power and propulsion in general. As long as we are limited to using chemical reactions to generate thrust, we have been, and will be unable to fly a single integral or unitary vehicle into orbit without shedding portions (or stages) in order to shed weight to allow vehicles to attain orbit. The power densities of rocket fuel/oxidizer combinations are so low that huge volumes of physical space must be used to contain chemical reactants. Thus, the great weight both of the propellants themselves, and of the very sizeable housing necessary to contain them and support the rest of the vehicle's mass, have left no alternative but "staging."

An artist's rendition of a SABRE powered spaceplane deploying a satellite to geostationary orbit.

Even as we continue to accelerate development of the Space Launch System (SLS) family of heavy-lift launchers, we will initiate two new projects for Earth-to-orbit operations. First, to gently and safely move humans and delicate hardware into and out of Earth orbit, we shall build a winged spaceplane using the revolutionary SABRE air-breathing rocket engines developed by Reaction Engines Ltd. in Britain (see *EIR* Vol. 45, No. 23, June 8, 2018). Work in this area is ongoing also in China, where world-leading hypersonic wind tunnels have been built, and in Russia. Military applications of the family of technologies around hypersonics and SABRE or combined-cycle (turbojet/ramjet/scramjet) engines, make cooperation in these areas difficult, but in the new atmosphere of a Four-Power agreement, countries may be more amenable to open collaboration.

Because this will be a first-of-a-kind project, knowledge shared across borders will be very important to successful attainment of this long-sought capability. As with other launcher systems, particular nations may wish to build their own spaceplanes, but each should at least have the advantage of shared research.

Secondly, we will initiate the development of the maglev launch system called StarTram. This high-risk/high-payoff proposal by Dr. James Powell, the developer of the superconducting maglev rail system being built now for regular passenger operation between Tokyo and Nagoya, Japan, has the potential to put 150,000 tons of supplies into low Earth orbit per year. Indeed, the experience of Japan, Germany and China in maglev development would make them very good candidates to take leading roles in this project.

StarTram will use buried superconducting coils to store up electrical energy over a long period, to be released in a short burst to accelerate a payload through a 100 km evacuated tube. The tube will curl 5,000 meters up a mountainside, allowing the spacecraft to proceed past the atmosphere, where a small chemical rocket burn can circularize its orbit. The first-generation system could launch twelve 40-ton spacecraft per day, each with a 35-ton payload. Thus, it could put 150,000 tons of supplies into orbit per year. This is the order of capability necessary to begin a permanent manned presence on the Moon or Mars.

By comparison, NASA's Space Launch System will initially have a 77-ton-to-orbit capacity, which will grow to a 143 ton-to-orbit capacity in the fully developed system. Even 1,000 launches per year (three a day) of the fully developed Space Launch System could not match the capability of the StarTram system.

StarTram, being completely different from all other space launch systems, poses high risk of failure,

Stratolaunch has built the largest plane in the world, from which it intends to launch spacecraft to orbit.

proved ease of access to LEO. Of note here are the efforts of SpaceX, Blue Origin, Sierra Nevada, Stratolaunch, and United Launch Alliance. A great deal of NASA's efforts will necessarily center on improving logistics. Every attempt to improve space logistics will be encouraged.

Even as we work on improving logistics-to-orbit and encourage participation from around the world, it is important to stress the need for agreement at the beginning on common measures, standards, fastener types, voltages, interfaces, docking systems, connectors, and so forth. It is not necessary to source each component from the same producer, but it is necessary that parts and modular components be capable of being recycled or repurposed from one space vehicle or building to another, without much need for modification. There will be many situations far from Earth in which one piece of equipment must be cannibalized to produce a part for something more critical to mission success.

We will also need a modular intermodal freight system. Like the Trailer Equivalent Unit (TEU) intermodal truck-rail-ship container system on Earth, we will need to configure a standardized container system for space. Especially for freight, we will want containers or pods which can detach from launchers, reattach

but will be a tremendous success if it can be made to function. However, it must be recognized that its 30 G acceleration in its tube, followed by a 6 G deceleration upon exiting the tube and entering the ambient atmosphere, makes the first-generation system suitable only for cargo. Of course, the demands for freight shipment to LEO, the Moon and eventually Mars will only continue to grow as the human presence in space spreads.

On the Moon, with no atmosphere, Ehricke had long ago proposed a simpler maglev launch system (no tube or tube endcap system required) to propel supplies with the relatively little energy required to attain lunar orbit from the Moon's surface. So, if we can get it to work on Earth, we will put a derivative on the Moon to easily catapult lunar-created materials (such as Helium 3 fusion fuel, water, hydrogen and oxygen) to orbiting spacecraft heading to Mars and points further out, or back to Earth.

At the same time that NASA is heavily committed to developing the revolutionary technologies mentioned above, it will continue to encourage and oversee the development of the private space transportation systems which have been evolving from chemical rocket technologies, but which use new approaches that offer the possibilities of somewhat lower operational costs per ton to orbit, and generally incrementally im-

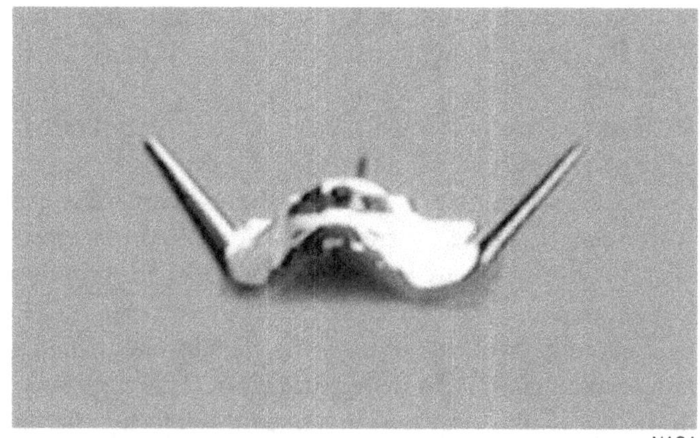

First drop-test flight at NASA's Dryden Flight Research Center of the Dream Chaser spacecraft from Sierra Nevada Corp.

SpaceX Falcon Heavy reusable boosters landing on pads 1 and 2 at Cape Canaveral, Florida.

to translunar or interplanetary tugs, and in some cases transfer to reusable landing craft at Moon or Mars orbit. More on this in a moment.

From Earth Orbit to Anywhere

Martian reconnaissance aside, any human development of Mars will be dependent upon the industrialization of the Moon. As Krafft Ehricke said, "If God had meant for Man to explore space, He would have given him a Moon!" So, we begin with the Moon.

Most of the initial exploration, prospecting, construction and operational activity will be accomplished by robotic systems. People will be primarily engaged in solving problems, making repairs and modifications, in future planning, and carrying out various kinds of research.

The ISS has established the important capability of recycling wastewater into drinking water. However, on the Moon, over time we will need to develop the ability to produce more and more of the food requirements of the lunar residents.

Since the lunar night lasts about two weeks, local solar food or solar power production is not even theoretically viable. Only nuclear fission, and later on, the even more energy-dense nuclear fusion power will suffice for powering lunar agriculture and other activity.

By 2070, we should expect that per capita energy consumption per person on Earth should be 1,000 times the level found in the United States today. In the settlements on the Moon, energy use per capita will be far greater—as the Moon will become the industrial center of the inner Solar System. It will not only yield the perfect fusion fuel, Helium-3, but also metals such as iron, aluminum, titanium and manganese, which are found here in greater general concentrations than are found on Earth. Combined with the 1/6th Earth gravity on the Moon, these metals make the Moon the ideal shipyard for spaceships and related hardware. But energy requirements will be extreme. To a certain extent, plentiful power can substitute for the deficiencies of habitability of the Moon. With enough power available, we can turn lunar regolith into the missing air and water we need.

Once an initial base site is chosen, robotic equipment will be sent to the site to begin producing supplies of water and its constituents, oxygen and hydrogen. Humans on the Moon will require protection from cosmic radiation and incoming meteorites. Therefore, other robotic equipment will begin to dig out access to underground caves, such as the long lava tubes discovered by Japan's JAXA SELENE orbiter, and install habitation modules there. Later, they will build lunar igloos around habitation modules placed on the surface along with power plants and basic infrastructure.

There is much room for innovation here, possibly using inflatable modules inside caves or igloos which are made of lunarcretes (lunar concretes). The idea is that we need at least some minimum of shielding from radiation and meteorites for the initial Moon base. Later on, we can develop a more sophisticated, active space defense system, but at the beginning, we will have to settle on passive shielding.

Here again, we have an example of a space problem whose solution solves a problem on Earth. Humans on Earth are threatened with the effects of collisions with large asteroids and comets. Humans on the Moon will be threatened by them as well, along with very tiny incoming particles. If we can create a lunar defense system to defend us against the tiniest incoming objects, then we can certainly figure out how to defend Earth from much smaller numbers of larger objects.

Human Transport Infrastructure

"Direct ascent" to the Moon was ruled out during the Apollo program, in favor of the successful Lunar Orbit Rendezvous approach. This meant that only a small Lunar Module went down to the lunar surface from lunar orbit, and then eventually returned to lunar orbit to rendezvous with the much larger Command Module. For the same reasons, the best approach to a deep space transportation system will be to separate out the Earth-to-Earth-orbit, Moon-to-Moon-orbit, and Mars-to-Mars-orbit processes, from the transfer processes between Earth orbit, Moon orbit and Mars orbit.

This means that out beyond low Earth orbit, we will need several specialized spacecraft. We already have the ISS in Earth orbit which can function as the initial Earth orbital spaceport.

We will need a lunar transfer vehicle or tug to operate between Earth orbit and lunar orbit. A lunar ascent/descent vehicle between the lunar surface and Moon orbit will also be needed (possibly using Krafft Ehricke's "slide lander" design).

To sustain people on Mars, we will need a corresponding set of vehicles with special characteristics.

It is important to note here that the relative closeness of the Moon to Earth, the relatively small gravity well, the presence of water and of Helium-3 fusion fuel, and the high concentrations of useful metals in the regolith make the Moon the ideal shipyard/refueling stop on the way out to anywhere.

Abundant potentials open up here, but the initial teams of astronauts, cosmonauts and taikonauts will site, oversee and coordinate the further introduction of robotic mining and processing facilities. Over time, oxygen, hydrogen, Helium-3, and eventually fabricated metal parts will be catapulted up to lunar orbit via the Ehricke maglev launcher mentioned above.

While the initial base is likely to be facing Earth, China's CNSA may wish to follow up on its Chang'e-4 lunar far-side astronomy work by further developing observatories on the lunar far side, away from Earth electromagnetic noise.

Along with wheeled vehicles, suborbital flying vehicles will be needed. As mentioned above, as much as possible, it were a good idea to design all of the relevant vehicles to be able to transport interchangeable freight or passenger containers—or pods. Every effort to simplify logistics will have a big payoff in the long run.

On to Mars

Beyond LEO, we will want to have an infrastructure that features continuously powered flight, as opposed to coasting on force-free trajectories as we do today. This is true of flight to the Moon, but it is more important for the long flight to Mars. Humans should not coast to Mars for months through the high radiation of deep

The Energy Density of Fuels

FUEL SOURCE	ENERGY DENSITY (J/g)
Combustion of Wood	1.8×10^4
Combustion of Coal (Bituminous)	2.7×10^4
Combustion of Petroleum (Diesel)	4.6×10^4
Combustion of H_2/O_2	1.3×10^4 (full mass considered)
Combustion of H_2/O_2	1.2×10^5 (only H_2 mass considered)
Typical Nuclear Fuel	3.7×10^9
Direct Fission Energy of U-235	8.2×10^{10}
Deuterium-Tritium Fusion	3.2×10^{11}
Annihilation of Antimatter	9.0×10^{13}

LaRouche PAC

As seen here, the energy density of nuclear fusion fuel is on the order of a million times that available in chemical fuels. The figure on page 17 of typical fusion fuels shows that the Helium-3 + Deuterium reaction gives the greatest energy output per reaction. More important is the fact that the reaction products do not include neutrons. This means that the reaction products can be controlled by magnetic fields, and that released neutrons do not cause unwanted transmutations in the surrounding machinery. This prevents unwanted derivative radioactive decay and consequent human and equipment health effects. Most important for spaceflight: the power of the charged products can be directly converted to electrical power. In other words, the relatively heavy and wasteful heat transfer to steam, to turbine, to generator can be bypassed. In technological progress in general, many areas of power production, transmission and use are moving away from heat-based processes to more efficient electromagnetic processes, as with maglev propulsion, fuel cells, or the light emitting diodes (LEDs) in your phone. This includes the space propulsion technologies, described in this article, which come under the general heading of Electric Propulsion.

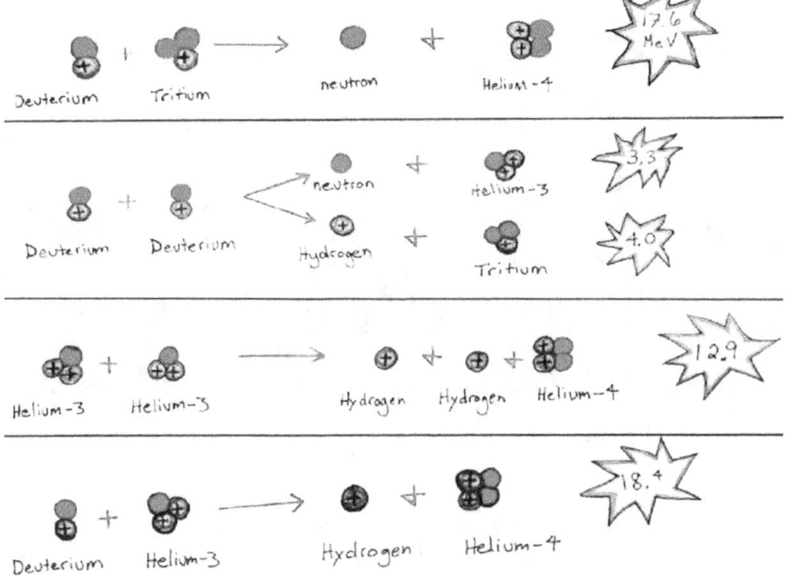

21st Century Science & Technology

Deuterium is plentiful in seawater. Helium-3, while rarely found on Earth, is found in relative abundance in the lunar regolith (and in even greater concentrations in the atmospheres of the Solar System's gas giant planets).

space. Even Columbus had sails to produce propulsion most of the time.

And this is not just a matter of radiation. The ISS has demonstrated the deleterious effects of long-term exposure of the human body to a zero gravity or microgravity environment. With continuous power, a continuous stress of some significant fraction of Earth's gravity—if not a full 1 G equivalent—can be maintained on the body. More research is necessary to determine the minimal sustained G force necessary to prevent deterioration of the human body, but the question becomes moot if we can develop a fusion rocket capable of sustaining a full 1 G acceleration.

This question was completely left open by the cancellation of the Japanese Centrifuge Accommodations Module of the ISS, (another X-38 situation) which might have given some clues to determination of a mini-

mum G level required to prevent deleterious biological effects. For now, we can say that our propulsion system should aim at achieving a full 1 G acceleration and deceleration—if possible. The closer we get to that, the more we reduce zero G and radiation risks to crews.

To achieve continuous power and thrust on the scale we really need, nuclear fission or fusion must be the ultimate source of power. In the inner solar system, where solar energy is usually plentiful, there are applications for solar power, but for power-dense requirements such as continuous propulsion over long distances at a significant acceleration, only a nuclear fission or fusion power plant will do.

The earliest designs for nuclear rockets, such as the NERVA project, replaced the heat and pressure created by burning chemical rocket fuel with the heating of an inert gas by a nuclear fission reactor. Such engines are called nuclear thermal rocket (NTR) engines. They produce about twice the specific impulse (the measure of impulse created per unit of propellant) of chemical rocket engines. These would be a great improvement, but still not likely to be able to produce the continuous thrust we would really want to provide people heading

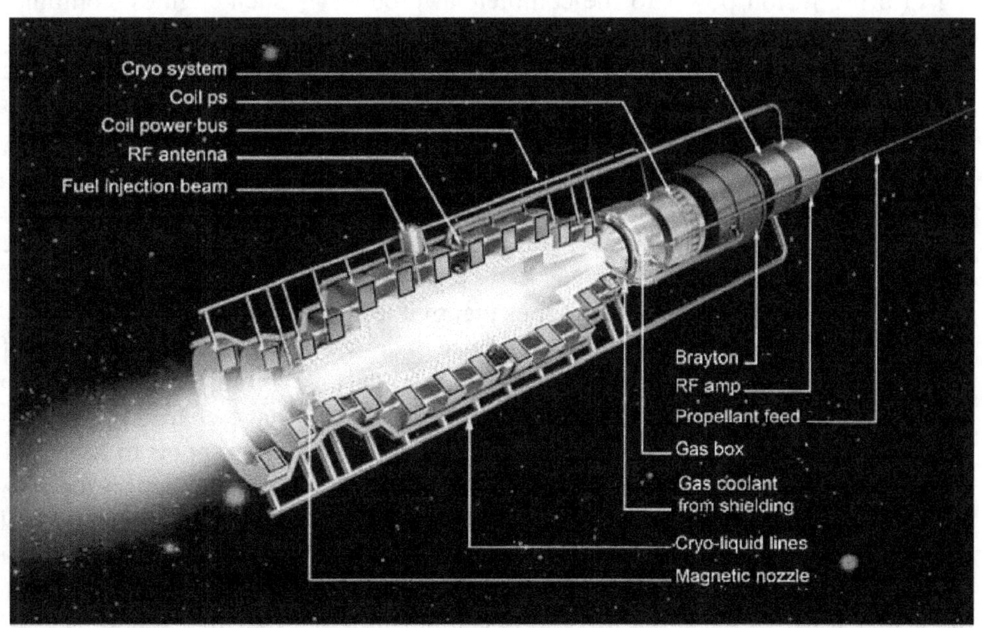

Princeton Satellite Systems

Artist's rendering of a Princeton Satellite Systems' Direct Fusion Drive engine, with interior cutout to show detail of the magnetic coils.

to Mars, for example.

NTR engines would perhaps suffice for the early development of the Moon. More likely solutions lie either in the realm of direct fusion rocket engines, or fission- or fusion-powered electric drives.

In 1980, Lyndon LaRouche, the Fusion Energy Foundation, and EIR News Service spearheaded a drive for a U.S. Government Man-

An artist's rendition of a VASIMIR engine test firing aboard the ISS.

hattan Project-style commitment to the development of a demonstration fusion power plant to be completed by the year 2000. The Magnetic Fusion Energy Engineering Act of 1980 was passed by Congress and was even signed into law by President Carter. However, the funding was sabotaged.

Nonetheless, although slowed, progress continued internationally. Today, besides the International Thermonuclear Experimental Reactor (ITER)—a giant experimental reactor under construction in France—and various government and university projects, commercially viable fusion applications are thought to be so near, that roughly a dozen private companies are working to bring fusion power to the commercial product stage.

Of special note here is the ongoing work at Lockheed Martin's Skunkworks. Unlike the giant ITER, the Skunkworks' efforts aim at producing compact fusion reactors capable of powering flight—among other uses.

Also, as we reported in the July 21, 2017 issue of *EIR*, Princeton Satellite Systems is developing what it calls the Direct Fusion Drive Engine.

With power densities a million times that of chemical combustion, such engines hold the promise of delivering the needed acceleration to reach Mars relatively quickly and with minimal ill effects upon a crew.

A second possibility lies in the area of what is called electric propulsion. Besides the superiority of Russian-built liquid-fueled engines in some areas (such as the RD-180 engine currently used by the American United Launch Alliance Atlas V first stage), Russia has been the leader for decades in the use and development of electric propulsion systems. Today, Russian electric propulsion systems are also typically found on American satellites. There are many variations in this area, but a typical electric propulsion system first ionizes an inert gas, and then uses electromagnetic acceleration of the ions out the rocket nozzle at significant fractions of the speed of light, in order to get very high impulse per ion—thereby achieving very high specific impulse values.

Unlike chemical rockets which create lots of thrust in a very short time, electric propulsion systems have generally been used until now for slow and steady jobs—like the station-keeping of geosynchronous satellites. However, this is also a function of the relatively weak electrical power available on satellites. Could such engines, combined with fission or fusion electric power generators, be clustered together in enough quantity to provide the continuous acceleration of a significant fraction of 1 G that we seek for human flight to Mars and beyond?

Former NASA astronaut and plasma physicist Dr. Chiang-Diaz and his Ad Astra Rocket Company have built an electric-drive engine called the Variable Specific Impulse Magnetoplasma Rocket (VASIMIR) engine. It uses many of the technologies developed in magnetic confinement fusion research machines, such as radio frequency heating of the plasma, and appears to have characteristics close to what we would want. In 2015, plans to test a 200-kilowatt version of the VASIMIR rocket on the ISS were cancelled (another X-38 situation). Soon we will have enough money to finally be able to test systems in space!

We should also mention here more "far out" schemes, whose operation is said to be impossible by the "laws of physics." We are speaking about strange theories of a propellant-less "Radio Frequency Resonant Cavity Thruster" or EmDrive, laser propulsion, space elevators, etc. Whether ludicrous or cutting edge, such theories need to be physically and rigorously tested. In the build and test process, the "laws of physics" will either be reinforced or rewritten. Either way, Man's power in the Universe is increased.

All of these dark-horse candidates, plus every likely successful concept of propulsion, whether Nuclear Thermal Rockets, the Direct Fusion Drive, or VASI-MIR, as well as every one of the multiple efforts at fusion power development, require the financial backup to be able to build and test in repeated cycles. We do not know which of the many efforts at solution to this problem will lead to practical space capabilities. We do know that accelerating this process will deliver the big payoff to the world economy. And we do know that the solutions are within sight.

Mars Itself

As better and better power/propulsion approaches are brought to fruition, and as we develop other technologies and capabilities in the process of lunar development, we begin to be able to plan for the founding of human operations on Mars. Mars is quite different from the Moon. It has a very thin atmosphere, which makes it seem more Earth-like. But, it is very far away from both the Earth and the Sun. One-way speed-of-light transmissions can take up to 20 minutes to reach Earth. This precludes assistance from ground controllers in emergency situations, as we have done on the Moon. Development of Mars will require much more autonomy and self-reliance than that of the Moon.

Mars colonization will have to build upon the successful solutions to the problems faced in lunar development. It will also benefit from the relatively cheap imports of metal parts and Helium-3 from the Moon. The very thin atmosphere composed mostly of carbon dioxide (great plant food!) suggests the possibility of martian agriculture in heated greenhouses (Mars is extremely cold).

Visionaries such as Lyndon LaRouche have long dreamed of "terraforming" Mars—potentially growing plants and forests on Mars. We shall see. As we get better and better control over the forces inhering in the atomic nucleus, we get better and better control of our Solar system.

The thin atmosphere also poses the possibility of the development of winged martian aircraft, both manned and robotic, to easily extend the reach of active operations. The ascent-descent vehicle for Mars will also have to be of a different design than the lunar ascent-descent vehicle because of its atmosphere.

Every aspect of human settlement on Mars is dependent upon successful attainment of fusion energy for propulsion and power. Otherwise it would be a dead end. But serendipitously, nearly every aspect of revolutionary progress on Earth is also dependent upon successful attainment of fusion power as the everyday underpinning of society. As we said at the beginning, the Moon-Mars project will properly organize the efforts of humanity on Earth to solve the problems on Earth. The spread of civilization into the Solar system could ironically just be thought of as a bonus byproduct!

Concluding Thoughts

Let us reiterate: Of course, we do not know in advance every particular of how this will all work out; much of it is still vague. It is left to the creative initiatives of people all over the world. There will be many advances beyond the bare outlines we have sketched here.

We *are certain* that someone and some nation must take the initiative to bring the future we seek into reality. We *are certain* that—for an array of historical and philosophical reasons—the world looks to the United States, with a restored Hamiltonian credit system, and NASA, to assume an initiating role in this process. We *are certain* that this will all more than pay for itself.

We do not go into space to get resources. We do not go to impress our neighbors. We do not go for immediate political advantages. We do not go to entertain the curious back on Earth. We do not go to win a race, for we shall all go together.

We take up this grand challenge as described in the immortal words of President Kennedy:

> We choose to go to the Moon … and do the other things, not because they are easy, but because they are hard, because that goal will serve to organize and measure the best of our energies and skills, because that challenge is one that we are willing to accept, one we are unwilling to postpone, and one which we intend to win, and the others, too.

China's Space Program: For the Common Destiny of Mankind

by Marsha Freeman

Oct. 18—The most dramatic changes in history are now taking place around the globe through China's Belt and Road Initiative. Countries that have long been denied access to modern technology are now becoming part of a web of transportation links, trade and commerce, and cultural exchanges that are reforming relations among nations. Central to the success of the Belt and Road projects will be the uplifting of populations through the application of the most advanced technologies and the scientific breakthroughs that create them. Space exploration will play a key role.

Speaking during the heads of space agencies session at the annual International Astronautical Congress (IAC) on Oct. 1 in Bremen, Germany, China National Space Agency (CNSA) Administrator Zhang Kejian said the conference's theme of inclusiveness is "coherent with China's policies. For example, the Belt and Road is supporting socioeconomic development, for the progress of human society." We should "join hands with other nations for the common destiny of mankind," he said.

Standing out among the world's space programs, is China's steadfast commitment to advancements in science and space technology, to be shared with developing nations, as subsumed under the Belt and Road Initiative. Recently, China has opened up its leading-edge manned and lunar space programs to international participation, with the focus on the nations that have not had access to space technology in the past. The New Silk Road, or Belt and Road Initiative, announced by President Xi Jinping in 2013, originally centered on cooperation with China's neighbors in Asia. Now, with more than 100 nations involved, the infrastructure, technology sharing, and cultural exchanges span virtually the entire world, from Asia to Europe, inclusive of Africa and Ibero-America.

Space exploration will play a leading role in the Chinese government's dedication to create the basis for future economic growth through scientific breakthroughs and technological innovation. China is offering those same opportunities to emerging space nations.

'A Common Home for all Humankind'

Two years ago, China's Manned Space Agency and the United Nations Office for Outer Space Affairs signed a Memorandum of Understanding to develop

NASA head Jim Bridenstine and Chinese National Space Agency head Zhang Kejian met on October 1 in Bremen, at the International Astronautical Congress. Both stressed the importance of U.S.-China space cooperation, for each country and globally.

the space capabilities of UN Members, using opportunities aboard China's upcoming space station. Member States were invited to submit proposals to conduct experiments aboard the station. On May 28 this year, an Announcement of Opportunity and instructions to apply for the program were released at a ceremony hosted in Vienna by the UN Office and the Permanent Mission of China to the United Nations.

The stated purpose of the initiative includes promotion of international cooperation in human space flight, and "capacity-building activities," by using human space flight technologies and resources from China's program. In what was described as "space diplomacy in action," Chinese Ambassador Shi Zhongjiun said at the ceremony: "The Chinese Space Station belongs not only to China, but also to the world.... Guided by the idea of a shared future, the [Chinese Space Station] will become a common home for all humankind. It will be a home that is inclusive and open to cooperation with all countries...."

On October 11, the UN Office, responding to a request for information from Andrew Jones of *Gbtimes*, reported that 36 teams from around the world had applied to send experiments to the station. The subject areas covered by the applications span virtually every aspect of space science, including asteroid redirection, astrophysics, plasma physics, space life science, Earth observation, and intelligent robots. UN and Chinese experts will evaluate the proposals over the next three months. The applicants selected will then have to submit implementation plans for the final selection.

China is planning to launch the first of three 20-ton modules to the station in 2020. The core module, called Tianhe (Harmony of Heaven), will house three astronauts, and carry their supplies for a stay of several months. The core module will control the station and provide the docking ports for up to three spacecraft at one time, to include visiting manned spacecraft and unmanned cargo ships. Over the following two years, two laboratories for scientific experiments will be added. The station will be able to carry more than 10 tons of scientific equipment and experiments. In addition to accommodating the experiments from the joint UN program, the station will also be open for use by China's bourgeoning commercial space companies.

For the past two years, officials working on China's

China Manned Space Agency

The completed Chinese space station is seen in this artist's rendering. The core module is central, with the flag. The two research laboratories are attached, with racks that are reserved for experiments from emerging space nations.

space station have stressed that the spacecraft has been designed to accommodate two additional modules that could be contributed by other nations, which are welcome to send their own crew members.

Regardless of what ultimately happens regarding the International Space Station (ISS), the Chinese space station should be operational by 2022, with the participation of countries that are optimistic about their future and have never been in space before.

As is perceptively pointed out by Mingyan Nie, from Nanjing University of Aeronautics and Astronautics, in a paper presented at the astronautical congress in Germany, "Concerning space affairs, they are in the majority hailed as instruments to attract more B&R [Belt and Road] participants and serve the other B&R programs' construction.... China actively makes use of its technological advantages," with the offer of sharing space technology, as an incentive for more countries to join the Belt and Road.

The Space Silk Road

In 1992, the Chinese government approved a manned space program, with the ultimate goal of an Earth-orbiting space station. The same year, China held the Asia-Pacific Workshop on Multilateral Cooperation

An artist's rendering of the Gaofen-5 Earth remote sensing satellite, launched on May 8, 2018. Note that its scientific instruments are pointed downward, toward the Earth.

in Space Technology Applications in Beijing for the first time, taking a leadership role in applying space technology for the development of the region. Out of that meeting came the creation of the Asia-Pacific Space Cooperation Organization. Its regional space activities are now being subsumed under China's Belt and Road Initiative.

Two years ago, China's space activities White Paper proposed the creation of the Belt and Road Space Information Corridor. Taking advantage of China's 200 Earth-orbiting satellites, the Corridor is intended to bring space-based technology into the service of economic and social development, and inform and aid major infrastructure projects of the Belt and Road. The Corridor is an information service, based on the use of data from communications, navigation, remote sensing, and science satellites. It is described as creating a public service platform for China's aerospace industry.

The Space Information Corridor serves two major purposes: connectivity among the Belt and Road nations, and satellite applications for development. First, satellite communication systems provide connectivity to isolated and underdeveloped regions, many with a difficult topography, such as mountains and deserts, which have little or no access to global or even national telephone or Internet communication, nor advanced education, scientific developments, or modern health care. Communication satellites can create a bridge to the most advanced modern technology.

When Earth-orbiting satellites were launched for the first time, mankind first saw the planet in three dimensions. Earth remote sensing technology has had a dramatic impact on nations' economies; on building infrastructure; locating and inventorying water resources; increasing the productivity of agriculture; forecasting extreme weather events; disaster recovery; and even human health.

In 2010, the government inaugurated the China High-resolution Earth Observation System—the CHEOS project. The task was to provide all-weather, 24-hour coverage using optical and radar satellites. A number of satellite constellations, each optimized for certain tasks, have been under development and are being deployed. China is sharing the data and images provided by those satellites. As space agency head Zhang reported at the Germany aerospace conference, "Joining with partners, China has provided 260,000 images to ASEAN [the Association of Southeast Asian Nations] and African states."

At the end of July, China launched the sixth in the series of Gaofen (meaning "high resolution") Earth remote sensing satellites, stating that the data will be used by the Belt and Road infrastructure initiative, in addition to domestic applications. The satellites in the Gaofen series carry instruments for multi-spectral imaging, and synthetic aperture radar, which sends pulses of radio waves toward the Earth and then measures the timing of the reflected signal. Geological features can be revealed, as can subsurface water resources. Unlike optical cameras, radar can "see" through clouds, and at night.

China's bourgeoning commercial space companies, most of which are spinoffs from China's giant state-owned aerospace enterprises, are actively engaged in marketing data from the commercial and government remote sensing satellites. Beijing Space View Technology Limited also operates a constellation of SuperView remote sensing satellites for Swei Star Company Ltd, which is a subsidiary of China Aerospace and Science Corporation. The objective of the SuperView minisatellites is to deliver panchromatic (essentially, black and white) images with a 0.5-meter resolution, and multispectral images with a lower 2-meter resolution. Last January, the second pair of SuperView satellites was launched. The completed constellation is designed to have 12 additional satellites by 2022.

But the goal is not just to provide ready-made images to emerging space nations, but also for them to have their own ground stations to receive the satellite data directly, and have the trained staff able to analyze and interpret, and present the data in a usable form to policymakers, farmers, urban planners, and others. To that end, China is deploying teams of specialists to create the necessary highly skilled workforce capable of tailoring data interpretation to other nations' specific needs.

Navigation and Positioning Systems

A third leg of the Space Silk Road, following communications and augmented remote sensing satellites, are navigation and positioning satellite constellations.

In 2000, China began the deployment of its Beidou satellite navigational system. One purpose was to end the Chinese military's reliance on the American Global Positioning System (GPS). Also considered were the many uses of navigational and positional data for the economy. The civilian applications of navigational satellites are critical for the projects along the Belt and Road corridors.

Positioning data are very useful for any mode of transportation, including cars, airplanes, and ships. Beidou satellites are being used for monitoring shipping in busy corridors, observing road traffic, and mapping and surveying land to determine routes for transportation projects, including road construction, and precise location and topography data for high-technology projects such as high-speed rail.

China is nearing completion of its Beidou satellite navigation system. The first series of satellites provided coverage of China. The second series, whose deployment will be completed this year, extends coverage across the Asian region of the Silk Road. By 2020, the third series of Beidou navigational satellites will establish global coverage. The completed third series constellation will consist of 35 satellites and will have a positioning accuracy of 2.5 meters. On October 15, China launched two third-generation Beidou satellites, with more planned for the remainder of this year.

Scientists are developing increasingly sophisticated applications for positioning technology. It was recently demonstrated that, using high-precision navigational satellite data, the slightest movement underneath a

A Beidou navigation satellite, covered by protective faring, is ready to be mated to its launch vehicle in 2016.

bridge or a dam that is under construction, such as soil subsidence, could be detected—avoiding a potential catastrophe.

The Space Silk Road provides the connectivity required for the construction of the multi-nation infrastructure projects underway, and, with future advancement in space technology, for the long-term economic growth of the Belt and Road nations.

The Next Frontier: The Moon

China has launched successful missions to orbit the Moon, land on the Moon, and direct a rover on its surface. In December, China will launch the Chang'e-4 spacecraft to land on the far side of the Moon. This has never been done before.[1]

Then, planned for 2020 is the Chang'e-5 mission to return samples of lunar soil to Earth, for intensive study of lunar chemistry and minerals, and of precious resources, such as the potential fusion fuel, helium-3, that have collected on its surface, deposited by the solar wind. In the following decade, China plans to begin a series of manned landings on the Moon. Cislunar transportation vehicles, living quarters, and other new infrastructure will be put in place.

As China's lunar program has progressed, it has

---

1. "China's Lunar Program Is Breaking New Ground," by Marsha Freeman, *EIR*, May 18, 2018, pp.11-14.

An artist's representation of a Moon base, the goal over the next decade of China's manned space program. Note the two astronauts on the lower left, for a sense of scale.

been increasingly opened to international participation. The Chang'e-4 lander, for example, houses a Low Frequency Spectrometer and Lunar Lander Neutrons and Dosimetry experiment, developed in Germany. At the IAC space conference, China's space agency head announced that on its lunar sample return mission, there are 10 kilograms of payload space being offered to other countries for their scientific experiments.

Next year virtually the entire world will celebrate the 50th anniversary of mankind's first landing on the Moon. That program was successful thanks to the forceful and consistent support from President Kennedy, a NASA Administrator who mobilized the resources, the astronauts who understood history was being made, and the more than a quarter of a million skilled workers, technicians, scientists, and engineers who brought it to fruition.

President Trump's first Space Policy Directive, released on December 11, 2017, directs NASA to "lead an innovative and sustainable program of exploration with commercial and international partners.... Beginning with missions beyond low-Earth orbit, the United States will lead the return of humans to the Moon for long-term exploration and utilization...."

China is following this path as we have seen.

China's space program will ultimately be successful because it is increasingly seen as a critical aspect of the Belt and Road Initiative, from youth being inspired to master science and engineering, through the practical applications of space technology, to new scientific discoveries resulting from missions of exploration.

Using "American methods" of federal credit and federal direction and support for great projects, and appreciating the success of that method in the Apollo program, China is leading projects that will change the face of much of the Earth through the Belt and Road, while opening deep space to human exploration.

In this regard, it would be wise for the United States to take a lesson from the Chinese and return to the American System economic policy of federal credit for infrastructure projects and support for science and technology research. Ensure the growth of the economy of the future through an educational system that has the goal of creating geniuses. Highlight for the public the fruits of science and research, and missions of challenge and exploration.

ZEPP-LAROUCHE ADDRESS

The New Silk Road, End of Colonialism: A New Shared Future for Humanity

Schiller Institute founder and President Helga Zepp-LaRouche keynoted an invitation-only event for diplomats and others in Washington, D.C. on Oct. 17. The event was also addressed by Virginia State Senator Richard Black, who spoke about the strategic situation in Syria, and former U.S. diplomat and foreign policy advisor to the Senate Republican leadership, James Jatras, who spoke on British interference in the United States from the Southern Confederacy to what the British call Russiagate.

Technical difficulties prevented recording the first few minutes of Zepp-LaRouche's remarks, in which she introduced the concepts of the new paradigm versus those of the old paradigm. The following is an edited transcript of her presentation.

Russiagate: Biggest Scandal in U.S. History

Now emerging and coming out into the open, is what will probably turn out to be the biggest scandal in the history of the United States—that is the so-called Russiagate and the so-called collusion of the Trump election campaign with Putin to win the election in 2016. This is all being exposed as collusion between the intelligence services of the Obama Administration with British intelligence—as a matter of fact, of MI6 and GCHQ with the FBI, the CIA, John Brennan, and the Department of Justice during the Obama Administration.

This is now all coming out into the open. There was, two days ago, a very fascinating interview with former U.S. Attorney Joseph diGenova on WMAL radio in Washington, in which he described how MI6 was conducting electronic surveillance on U.S. citizens at the request of the FBI, and CIA Director Brennan. Brennan actually visited London and he met with MI6 and GCHQ before the whole Russiagate story began, and where this all started still needs to be clarified. Did it come from John Brennan or did it not come from Brit-

CIA

Former U.S. Attorney Joseph diGenova (left) exposes electronic surveillance on U.S. citizens done at request of the FBI and CIA Director John Brennan (above).

ish intelligence? This question is now opening up. According to diGenova, who is the former U.S. Attorney for Washington, D.C., this is a tremendous liability on the part of these U.S. intelligence officials—for possible criminal prosecution.

It is also very clear that President Trump is completely aware of the coup against him, and that he is planning to defeat it. As a matter of fact, he just was in a very remarkable interview for "60 Minutes" with

Lesley Stahl, where afterwards Lesley Stahl commented that he is now fully in control, that he is now running his Presidency in a completely sovereign way. And when she, in the interview, asked him if he would pledge that he would not get rid of the Mueller investigation, he said, "I don't have to pledge anything to you. I'm the President, and you are not."

So, it is very clear that Trump has defeated the Mueller investigation, which is now practically over. We are now three weeks from the Nov. 6 election, and a lot can happen in between. For example, you could have sudden turns, you could have a new financial crash much bigger than the one of 2008. We could also have the complete declassification and publication of all the documents related to this British coup against an American President. If that comes out, then it will not only be the biggest scandal—that the so-called "closest ally" of the United States, Great Britain, was involved in a coup attempt against an elected President—but this will reveal the motives, why this attempted coup occurred.

And that goes immediately to Trump's promise in the election campaign that he would remedy the relationship with Russia. As you could see in the very successful summit he conducted in Helsinki with President Putin, despite the incredible stories thrown against him with the Russiagate story, he is, indeed, on this course. Not only will the British role come out, but also the different British operations, the false flag operations against the Syrian government, which Virginia State Senator Richard Black talked about, and naturally also, the phony Skripal affair. All of the British operations were designed to draw the United States into an increasing confrontation against Russia.

From recent encounters we've had in the United States with people at the Trump rallies, and also with

DoD/D. Myles Cullen

NATO Supreme Allied Commander in Europe Gen. Curtis Scaparrotti says the West is already at war with Russia.

simple citizens in the streets, it is very clear that Americans increasingly understand that this is a coup against the President.

The polarization in the United States, right now, as you all are aware, is unprecedented. And what is really clear is that the Democrats are in an all-out effort in the midterm election to win the House of Representatives, and possibly pick up some Senate seats. They have on their agenda,— if they win, they will probably be able to lure some neo-con Republicans into their camp and go for an immediate impeachment of President Trump.

If that were to happen, we would be immediately back on a path to war against Russia and against China. Look at the very bellicose statements, for example, by General Curtis Scaparrotti, NATO Supreme Allied Commander in Europe, who recently said that the West is already at war with Russia, that it's not yet a shooting war, but they are at war. The Democrats have been the real war party, in the recent period, even beyond what Obama and Hillary Clinton were doing in their time. With the Democrats back in power, we would be back on a confrontation with Russia right away.

It is also very doubtful, if there were to be any power play in this election, that the Trump supporters would take it. So, we are in for a really, very decisive battle, in which world peace depends on Trump getting the necessary backing. Trump people in the United States immediately freak when you say that, but it is the case.

Now, what is the understanding of this internal situation in the rest of the world? Well, it is very clear from the statement of different Russians, like Foreign Minister Lavrov, for example, that the Russians have a quite differentiated view. They do know what President Trump is up against— they always make a clear distinction between what Trump says and what the Senate says, as does China.

Xinhua/Dai Tianfang

Russian Foreign Minister Sergey Lavrov.

The Chinese right now are really quite disappointed with the Trump Administration's tariff policy, and even feel outright anger because, after the initial very positive relations between Trump and Xi Jinping, their relations are really not on the level they should be right now as a result of this. Nevertheless, they make a big distinction between such outrageous attacks on China, coming from Pence and also Bolton, and on the other side, Pompeo and General Mattis, who frequently just said that it is not the intention of the United States to contain China.

CC/Gage Skidmore

Steve Bannon

In Europe, it is absolutely amazing. I just checked this afternoon to be sure, and my colleagues confirmed for me that practically in no European country has there been honest coverage of this coup attempt. Articles, when they do appear, are rare, and if they mention anything at all about Christopher Steele, they never mention the British role as such! Such references are so opaque that nobody can understand them who has not got a complete knowledge of the whole story; and the other references are spins, attacks on Trump, and generally take the side of the Democrats. It is quite amazing that in Europe, concerning an issue where world peace is at stake, people are really in the dark.

mendous stealing of technologies—which by the way, is a lie, because China, in the meantime, has long surpassed the state of its development where it was dependent on stealing technology, and has become a leading power in many areas of science and technology itself.

Now, ever since Xi Jinping announced the New Silk Road in Kazakhstan in 2013, about 100 countries have joined this effort. There have been investments in all of these countries, totaling 12 times the size of the Marshall Plan, all based on a win-win cooperation—an enormous number of infrastructure corridors, industrial parks, power plants; various agricultural projects have been built. And in the recent time, you have the building of a completely new system of international relations, based on respect for sovereignty, respect for noninterference in the affairs of the other country, and respect for the perspective of different social systems, and this has created a completely different dynamic in the world.

This has, for example, recently led to the complete integration of the Shanghai Cooperation Organization with the Belt and Road Initiative. There is a new formation of South-South relations which became very apparent at the recent annual BRICS meeting in Johan-

Thucydides Trap or New Silk Road?

The big question other than this internal fight in the United States, is the conflict between the United States and China. It is the old question of the "Thucydides trap": How will the up-to-now dominant power, namely the United States, react to a secondary power rising and eventually bypassing it? What are people such as Steve Bannon and Kissinger, who seem to have formed an alliance, and many think tanks, so absolutely freaked out about? Bannon is absolutely obsessed. He says that China represents a mortal danger to the existence of the United States, that there is a tre-

Xinhua/Wang Ye

Opening of the Beijing Summit of the Forum on China-Africa Cooperation (FOCAC) in the Great Hall of the People in Beijing, Sept. 3, 2018.

nesburg, where you had the formation of Global South, which was practically all the organizations from the developing sector, the G77, the Organization of Islamic Cooperation, Mercosur, the African Union, many regional organizations. And then the very big Africa-China summit, of the Forum on China-Africa Cooperation (FOCAC), in Beijing at the beginning of September, at which about 48 presidents and 5 other heads of state or government participated from Africa, announcing a new era in the friendship and relations between China and the countries of the African continent.

The Holhol Bridge on the Standard Gauge Addis Ababa-Djibouti Railway.

At the BRICS summit, Russian President Vladimir Putin promised that Russia would light up Africa by providing electricity, not from oil and gas, but through helping African nations to build nuclear power plants. At the same meeting, Xi Jinping said that Africa, of all the places in the world, has the biggest development potential in the world.

Now the New Silk Road Spirit, which has really captured this dynamic, is transforming geopolitical conflicts in many parts of the world. For example, the very successful developments concerning North and South Korea, who are now fully on the way to possibly announcing a peace treaty before the end of the year, and going in the direction of unification. This is definitely one of the great successes of President Trump, who at the Singapore summit with North Korea's Kim Jong-un, promised to help to make North Korea a prosperous country if the denuclearization continues. And China has promised to integrate the Koreas into the Belt and Road Initiative. Russia has also promised to contribute to the economic prosperity in North Korea. This is a model in which you can see how this new spirit is helping to transform previous crisis situations into real miracles.

A similar thing is happening in the Horn of Africa where—as a result of the construction of the fast railway between Djibouti and Addis Ababa—Somalia, Djibouti, Eritrea and Ethiopia are now developing new diplomatic relations and cooperation, which was unthinkable a very short time before.

The biggest breakthrough in such developments occurred two days ago with the signing of a Memorandum of Understanding between the Italian government and the Lake Chad Basin Commission on the realization of the Transaqua project. The LaRouche organization has been fighting for Transaqua for over 30 years.

That China, Italy and six African nations have agreed to build it, is a game-changer for the entire African continent. Transaqua will refill Lake Chad, which is now down to about 10% of its previous volume, by bringing 3-4% of the water from the tributaries of the Congo River in a region about 500 meters higher, through a system of canals, into Lake Chad, creating an inland waterway for participating countries. It will provide hydropower, it will provide huge amounts of water for irrigation, it will fill up Lake Chad, and it will still provide for large areas in the Sahel zone to be irrigated. And that way you can really improve the life about 40 million people who live there.

This is a tremendous breakthrough, and I think this is really the kind of project which can happen around the world everywhere.

In the context of the New Silk Road, there have also been an enormous number of strategic realignments of countries that previously, for historical reasons and past wars, were completely at odds. For example, now there is a new cooperation between Japan and China, where both say that there is the possibility of joint projects in Africa. Prime Minister Shinzo Abe, just two days ago, said that Japan and China can cooperate in third countries and the pivot could be Thailand. Another great project, for which we have been fighting for more than 30 years, is the Kra Canal, about which there has recently been a conference putting that project back on the agenda. The Kra Canal would be a game-changer for the entire transport route in Southeast Asia.

Even as Latin American countries are extremely keen to work with China, U.S. Vice President Pence had threatened them and attacked them, saying they shouldn't cooperate with China. But, since the United States is not offering what China is offering, the tendency is clearly in this direction.

In Europe, the reaction has been mixed. The European Union and Berlin are insisting on a "European way." I'll come to what that means in a second. Tomorrow is the Asia-Europe Meeting (ASEM), in Brussels, where the Europeans will propose their own connectivity as a counter to the New Silk Road, but China so far sees no problem in such an arrangement, saying the two schemes can be integrated. Let's see what happens at this summit.

But even Europe is completely captured by the advantages of cooperating with the New Silk Road. The 16+1, the Central and Eastern European countries (CEEC) plus China, are bringing in lots of infrastructure projects, and this has instilled optimism, for example in the Visegrad countries—that is Poland, Czech Republic, Slovakia and Hungary— whose transport ministers just met and announced that they want to connect their capitals through high-speed rail systems. So soon the Visegrad countries will be more prosperous and have more advantages than the West European countries which have basically not engaged in such infrastructure projects.

A wonderful example of cooperation with the New Silk Road is Austria, where Chancellor Sebastian Kurz will conduct a big Europe-Africa Forum, before the end of the year. Austria has the presidency of the Eu-

Japanese Prime Minister Shinzo Abe.

UN/Cia Pak

kremlin.ru

Austrian Chancellor Sebastian Kurz.

Xinhua/Cheng Tingting

Italian Under Secretary of State Michele Geraci

ropean Union for this present half-year; many institutions in Austria and Vienna are completely enthusiastic. For example, the head of the Vienna Chamber of Commerce is pushing for the complete integration of Austria into the New Silk Road. And he said the New Silk Road is very easily explained: It is our economic future. The Mayor of the city of Linz called the connection of Austria to China the "Trade Route of Creativity."

Also the new Italian government, which is being attacked by the mainstream media practically every day, is practically going for a full strategic alliance with China. Various cabinet ministers, Michele Geraci, and Giovanni Tria just returned from China after concluding huge deals, inviting China to rebuild Italy's infrastructure. Paolo Savona, made a wonderful speech in the Italian Chamber of Deputies, comparing Italy's new economic plan to Franklin D. Roosevelt's New Deal, and also advocating cooperation between China and Italy in Africa. And before the Transaqua Memorandum of Understanding, there was an earlier memorandum of understanding between China and Italy to engage in this great project. So this can be a model of any Western country.

This plan is also, naturally, coming under attack by the European Council on Foreign Relations, which is a George Soros-financed institution. I think the Swiss financial daily *Neue Zürcher Zeitung* summed it all up recently, writing about Europe's "paralyzing fear of Africa," pointing to the crucial difference that Europeans only see Africa as a source of refugees, as a big migration crisis, while China is seeing the economic opportunity, and that therefore Europe is completely missing the signs of the times; that even countries including India, Turkey, the Gulf States, Russia, Brazil, Indonesia, Thailand, Japan, and China, all are saying, "Let's go to Africa; this is where the economic next big development will take place." These people are talking about Africa being a "new China with African characteristics."

A New Paradigm for the Old

Now, the new paradigm is very clearly a new system of relations among nations, which allows the developing countries to leapfrog, overcome their underdevelopment, and get access to advanced technology. The old paradigm is completely hysterical about that, because if you look at what they have been trying to build, especially after the collapse of the Soviet Union, namely, a unipolar world based on the "special relationship" between the United States and Great Britain, they're trying to save what Zbigniew Brzezinski called the "Great Game," the efforts to contain Russia and China.

PNAC, the Project for a New American Century, was put on the agenda by the neo-cons after the collapse of the Soviet Union— going for "humanitarian" interventions; causing wars in the Middle East under the pretext "right to protect"; going for regime change, in which Syria is just one example—Iraq, Libya, other situations. All this has created a situation in which the developing countries have increasingly realized that they have to do something.

After the Asian crisis—already a result of the economic policies associated with this old paradigm— when George Soros speculated against the currencies of Southeast Asian countries in one week, driving their value in respect to the U.S. dollar down 50, 60, 80%, they realized they had to do something to defend themselves. The first such step was the Chiang Mai Initiative, an effort to protect against speculative attacks; and then came the Contingent Reserve Arrangement as a part of the BRICS policy, another effort in the same direction. But then, especially, the financial institutions associated with the New Silk Road—the Asian Infrastructure Investment Bank, the New Silk Road Fund, the Maritime Silk Road Fund, and many others—all created specifically to provide financing of infrastructure.

Now the old paradigm was not just something with respect to the so-called "advanced sector," but it was a paradigm shift at the end of the 1960s, ending the relative industrial optimism of the Kennedy period, the de Gaulle and Adenauer period, by trying to go to a post-industrial utopia. At that time the Club of Rome appeared with its fraudulent *Limits to Growth* theory, which was the idea that you had strict limits to raw materials, that you had to basically go for austerity, and this was a complete fraud. It was admitted by Meadows and Forrester, the authors, later on, namely, that they had left out completely the role of science and technology in defining what a "raw material" is.

Along the same line, the famous or infamous, Kissinger-authored National Security Study Memorandum 200 (NSSM-200), came out in 1974, which guided U.S. foreign policy, saying that all raw materials belong to the United States and therefore excessive world population growth should be curbed because too many people will need too many raw materials. At that time, there was the promotion of a concern for the so-called "population explosion" as the biggest threat to world stability, and they developed the ideas of "sustainable development" and "appropriate technology," which really meant *no* technology, because "appropriate technology" means everybody gets a shovel and can dig their own fields, but no tractors, no advanced machinery. NSSM-200 was only declassified sometime in the 1990s.

At the same time, you had the World Wildlife Fund under the leadership of Prince Philip, on behalf of this same British Empire, blocking any kind of development project in the developing sector.

The policies of the World Bank have to be critically reviewed in this context, because many of the loans given for development projects were organized in such a way that they had to be repaid even before the project had yielded any real productive result; the World Bank

We have 12 years to limit climate change catastrophe, warns UN

Urgent changes needed to cut risk of extreme heat, drought, floods and poverty, says IPCC

Overwhelmed by climate change? Here's what you can do

▲ A firefighter battles a fire in California. The world is currently 1C warmer than preindustrial levels. Photograph: Ringo HW Chiu/AP

The world's leading climate scientists have warned there is only a dozen years for global warming to be kept to a maximum of 1.5C, beyond which

never financed infrastructure as the needed framework for these projects. That approach went along well with the infamous IMF conditionalities, conditionalities which prevented investment in infrastructure or even social systems in the developing sector, by demanding that debt repayment had priority over any domestic investments. This is the reason why there has been such a tremendous deficit in infrastructure.

This is also what the EU means when they say that the development of Africa needs to be "sustainable," "appropriate." They still have not woken up to the fact that what Africa and all the developing countries need, is real investment in infrastructure, in industry, in science and technology, in the most advanced technologies.

IPCC Turns Up the Heat of Dangerous Nonsense

Now recently, when it became clear that the New Silk Road was developing an unbelievable dynamic, there came renewed, unprecedented attacks, this time from the Intergovernmental Panel on Climate Change (IPCC) demanding the total decarbonization of the world economy by the year 2050. This is an old-hat project of John Schellnhuber, the former president of the Potsdam Institute for Climate Impact Research, who in 2011 published a report called the *World in Transition—*

Social Contract for a Great Transformation, demanding exactly the total decarbonization of the whole world's economy.

Many countries are completely dependent on coal, and that will not change for a long time, until we have developed new levels of energy, like fusion power.

Now we have demonstrated, and Schellnhuber has also admitted, or even demanded, that if you go to a complete decarbonization of the world economy, the carrying capacity of the Earth is about 1 billion people. In his "60 Minutes" interview, Trump basically dismissed the IPCC report, and said he was not going to spend billions of dollars and destroy millions of jobs for an unproven change in the climate; that there is absolutely no scientific proof that the climate change that is taking place is caused by man's activity.

Indeed, climate change has been going on for millions of years in cyclical fashion—ice ages, warming trends—which are mostly caused by the position of our Solar System in the galaxy, and all the causes have not been researched sufficiently to demand such incredible demands such as the decarbonization of the economy, which would lead to a dramatic collapse—as a matter of fact, it would be genocidal in its effects.

Energy Flux-Density and Progress

One of the unique contributions of my husband, Lyndon LaRouche, was to develop the absolute connection between the potential relative population density on the planet and the energy flux-density in the production process. Each qualitative breakthrough is associated with a breakthrough in the energy flux-density, thus defining a new economic platform. If you look at the upward development from using combustion of wood as an energy resource, to combustion of coal, petroleum, natural gas, nuclear fission, and—on the horizon—fusion, then you can see that with these increases in energy flux-density you have an absolute rise in the potential of the Earth to maintain more people, living longer lives and in better conditions.

Now energy flux-density can be measured by the rate of energy use per person and per unit area of the economy as a whole. The energy used with a 2,000 calorie diet per person in civilization as it existed before man was able to tame fire for production uses, was about 100 watts, where every activity depended on the muscle of human beings. When the leap occurred to a wood-based economy, it comes to 3,000 watts per person, a 30-fold increase. With coal as a combustible fuel, it is 5,000 watts; with petroleum, the per capita rate of energy consumed shot up to 10,000 watts, which is already over 100 times that of a society without fire.

If nuclear fission were to become the dominant energy source, we would arrive at 20,000 watts per person, which would provide a much higher living standard and greater longevity for everyone, comparable to the best living standards in the United States and Western Europe today.

But this improvement of living standards is exactly what the neo-liberal oligarchy of the old paradigm wants to deny the developing countries. Just remember the disgusting speech given by President Barack Obama in his trip to South Africa, in which he said, if everybody in Africa wants to have a car, air conditioning, and a big house, the planet will boil over. Now, this open racism should never be forgotten. "Sustainable development" means "no development," and it is really very useful that President Trump rejected the IPCC report.

I have not yet seen if there was any reaction coming from China, which previously only criticized the impossibility to implement the required measures, but to my knowledge China has not questioned in general the unscientific basis for this report. I have not yet seen the Russian reaction, either. But I remember very well that at the Copenhagen climate conference in 2009, it was the Sudanese head of the G-77, Lumumba Di-Aping, who refused to accept the findings of that climate conference, saying, "We are not going to sign a suicide pact."

Now, if the New Silk Road becomes the World Land-Bridge, which is exactly what is in the process of happening, then in the next one to two generations, the world will require a completely new economic platform, in the terms it has been defined by LaRouche. It will require at least a tenfold increase in energy production and consumption, and obviously an immediate crash program for fusion power.

The IPCC report, in a scandalous way, says that they intend to invest $122 trillion by the year 2050, to implement the decarbonization of the world economy, and since these people are anti-nuclear as well, you go only to renewables—wind, solar, and so forth. If you were to

FDR Library

President Franklin Roosevelt at the Boulder Dam, 1935.

invest the same sum, or even less, in fusion power, the breakthroughs could be accomplished in the near future.

Xi Jinping has set a different goal for 2050. He said, in the next development phases of the cooperation of all these countries participating in the New Silk Road, you will have by 2050 a completely new, beautiful, and wonderful world for the entire human population. This is an absolutely reachable goal. If you just consider that the wealth of only one man, Jeff Bezos, the owner of Amazon, whose private wealth is $150 billion, would be enough to pay for clean water for the entire world's population for 15 years, you can see how quickly the approach taken by the New Silk Road countries can actually lead to this result.

Lyndon LaRouche's Four Laws

What you need is the entire Four Laws program by Lyndon LaRouche: You need Glass-Steagall banking separation in the tradition of Roosevelt's 1933 Banking Act. You need that on a global scale, which means you have to end the casino economy.

You have to go, secondly, to the American System of economy, a national banking system in the tradition of Alexander Hamilton. And you have to create a New Bretton Woods system, an international credit system, by which countries cooperate with national banking systems that provide credit for production, for real investment in the real economy, the most recent examples being the Reconstruction Finance Corp. of Franklin D. Roosevelt and the Kreditanstalt für Wiederaufbau, the

Credit Institution for Reconstruction, used by Germany in the postwar period to bring about the German economic miracle. Were the banks in the West reorganized according to this model, they could then cooperate with the AIIB, the New Silk Road Fund, and others, for fulfilling the World Land-Bridge.

And especially, you would need the Fourth Law of LaRouche, which is a crash program for fusion power and international cooperation in space to achieve a massive increase in the productivity of the world economy. Now, space research and travel are especially important because they uplift the eyes and minds of the people to our larger universe, and they make clear that the idea of our planet being a closed system is completely ludicrous. Consistent with space exploration and the fact that our planet conforms to the laws of the universe, which are anti-entropic, a new economic platform will be established, and many further ones are already visible.

My husband Lyndon LaRouche said many years ago, that the only way this will get done is if the four most important powers—the United States, Russia, China, and India—work together to implement a New Bretton Woods system, because only they have the power to undo the present system of financial control of Wall Street and the City of London.

Obviously, now, most people will ask: "Is that possible? Can the world be persuaded to join the new paradigm?" Well, provided the midterm elections turn out well for President Trump, it is my biggest hope and firm expectation that we will be much freer in the second half of his first term, and that he will pursue positive relations with Russia, and that if he meets with President Xi Jinping, that they will find a way to overcome the present tariffs crisis in a better way than implementing additional and higher tariffs, which are really driving both sides into lose-lose positions.

Great Power Cooperation in Earth's Next 50 Years

If Japan and China can cooperate in third countries for their mutual benefit, I think the United States and China can do so. For example, the United States could accept Chinese investments in building up the infrastructure of the United States, connecting all the major cities where infrastructure is currently in such terrible condition. If you drive from Washington to New York, you'll find that the highways are full of potholes. The railroads are in terrible condition. The United States has *no* fast train system at all, while China is connecting *all* its major cities with fast train systems by 2035. That could be done in the United States.

And the United States could make joint ventures in third countries in collaboration with China, rather than threatening Latin America not to cooperate with China. The United States and China should develop together the Latin American continent. They could invest in Asia; together they could develop Africa—a huge continent, which needs international cooperation. The trade deficit can be overcome by making trade bigger.

There is a new concept of great power relations, developed by China, and proposed to the United States. In light of the current tensions between China and the United States, the *Global Times*, a government-related newspaper, recently asked the question: "What should the relations be between China and the United States in 30, 40, 50 years from now, or even towards the end of the century?"

In 2005, my husband Lyndon LaRouche wrote a beautiful book called *Earth's Next Fifty Years*, in which he developed the absolutely optimistic perspective that the future of Eurasia, and by implication the rest of the world, should be dominated by the ideas of Vladimir Vernadsky, namely that the noösphere will play an increasingly dominant role over the biosphere. That is, that the impact of human creativity, of inventions in scientific and technological breakthroughs, will increasingly dominate the behavior of human beings, and will constitute a physical force in the universe.

Now, I think that is absolutely what our true identity should be: The human species is the only known creative species in the universe, at least the only one known so far, and this is a moment when I think we have to grow up as human beings and become truly human. We cannot sit on the sidelines of history in such a moment.

I would like to remind you of what Schiller said in "What Is Universal History and Why Does One Study It?" He said—and I am saying it now in my own words—We should look at the long chain of generations before us, who gave us a tremendous heritage. Should it not be our proud and passionate desire to connect our ephemeral life to that long chain of human generations, and contribute with our own life, so that soon, a generation will be living a better life as a result of what we have done?

So, in this period, in the words of Schiller, there is one thing to be done worth speaking of, so let's do it. Thank you.

Italy Promotes the FDR Model, Repudiates Austerity

by Claudio Celani

Oct. 18—If you want to know why the City of London, EU headquarters in Brussels, the European Central Bank (ECB) in Frankfurt and chancellorships in Paris and Berlin are so hysterical about the new Italian government, you'll find the answer in the speech that Minister of European Affairs Paolo Savona, the most senior member of the Italian government, made in Parliament Oct. 11. Savona announced that Italy proposes to go back to Franklin Delano Roosevelt and his New Deal, as a policy model. That statement is being read as a declaration of war by the European oligarchies.

Italy's Plan Challenges EU Austerity

In presenting the Economic and Financial Planning Package, the *Documento di Economia e Finanza* (DEF) for the next three years to Parliament, Savona said that he personally would have liked to spend much more than the planned 2.4% of GDP, but the decision was taken to proceed with "prudence" and nevertheless demonstrate that investments and not austerity improve fiscal stability. Savona's speech, in Italian, is available at https://www.youtube.com/watch?v=tGP4XhLX6Pk.

The planned Italian budget deficit, as presented by Savona, is a violation of EU rules, according to which "indebted" countries such as Italy must converge on a balanced budget by cutting the deficit every year. Italy has adhered to that policy for decades, with the result that the country has plunged into a severe depression, with over 5 million poor and a real unemployment figure close to twenty percent.

The new budget envisions measures to alleviate poverty, provide tax relief for small and medium-sized enterprises (SMEs) and free resources for investments in order to achieve a planned 1.4% GDP growth in 2019.

Franklin D. Roosevelt Library

President Franklin D. Roosevelt (above) greets enthusiastic supporters in Warm Springs, Ga., on Dec. 1, 1933.

Paolo Savona, Italian Minister of European Affairs.

CC/Filippo Vilani

In his presentation in the Chamber of Deputies, Savona explained:

I must greatly insist on the fact that it is necessary to replicate, a hundred years later, what Roosevelt did with the New Deal and his reforms. He put together the industrialized part of the northern United States with the southern agricultural part—which had serious racist-based problems—and he succeeded. Therefore, it is my belief that the experiment we are conducting in this moment is really a large effort of national unity, of coincidence between the interests of the advanced and the backward—economically speaking—parts of the country.

The conclusions of the DEF are clear: it is an ambitious program and we are aware of that; but the New Deal program was ambitious too, even if in a different context.... It aims at responding to the increase of poverty since the [breakout of] the crisis especially among youth and large families, and in the southern regions of the country.

We all agree that the country needs investments. Therefore, let us start to build a New Deal.... But, the government program is very prudent, because we are aware that we must implement those reforms that Roosevelt started. Roosevelt made a substantial reform in the financial sector, on competition, on industrial relations [read: Glass-Steagall, anti-trust legislation, pro-labor reforms]. Those who know history ... know that he made very important initiatives.

Savona pointed to the fact that Italy's trade balance has produced 50 billion Euros per year of savings surplus, a surplus which is not used. This defines a potential of up to 150 billion for the next three years, the span covered by the DEF, which could be used for investments. Italy is living "below its resources, contrary to what they say, especially at European level," Savona said. The government plans to increase investments by one, four and then five percent in the next three years; yet, nevertheless, critics call this "unfeasible" and illusory.

The fact that Savona was chosen to represent the government in the vote on the budget outline has a high political significance. Usually it would be the Finance Minister to do so, but Giovanni Tria was at an IMF meeting in Bali. Tria could have been represented by one of his deputies—or even by the Prime Minister, given the importance of the matter. The choice of Savona is a nice little revenge against those—at European level—who had vetoed his original nomination as Finance Minister, recognizing that even with a "ministry without portfolio," as Minister of European Affairs, Savona is nevertheless being called upon to play a key role in the government.

His speech was interrupted several times by strong applause, culminating in his request for a glass of water and his remark: "I drink water." Everybody saw a reference to EU Commission chairman Juncker, one of his opponents and a notorious boozer.

The Chamber approved the DEF with 331 votes against 191, the Senate with 161 against 109.

EU Rejection: What Does It Mean?

The Italian plan must now get the approval of the EU Commission, which has already announced that it will reject it and demand "corrections." However, when arriving at an EU summit Oct. 17, Prime Minister Giuseppe Conte told journalists that "there are no margins" for corrections.

EU institutions and leaders are split on how to deal with Italy. On one side, the hawkish faction wants to break Italy with a combination of political and financial warfare, in order to force it drop its plans and submit to the Troika (EU Commission, ECB and IMF), which would impose an even more brutal austerity regime. This faction—according to Reuters, which quoted a "high ECB official"—is ready to block Emergency Liquidity Assistance to Italian banks, similar to what they did in 2015 to force Greece to accept the Troika.

That scenario would start with rating agencies downgrading the Italian sovereign debt, causing a run on Italian bonds and a dramatic rise in refinancing costs for the Italian government. This in turn, would create a banking crisis, as Italian banks would be forced to replace such bonds with new capital or face insolvency.

A foretaste of this scenario was provided when an Oct. 5 letter sent by EU Commissioners Vladis Dombrovskis and Pierre Moscovici to the Italian government in fact did unleash a mini-run on Italian bonds, increasing the spread between Italian and German bonds to 300 points. A level of 400 points is considered to be unsustainable for Italian banks.

A second letter by the same duo, hand-delivered by Moscovici in Rome Oct. 18, rejected the Italian budget proposal as "a particularly serious non-compliance with the [Stability] Pact's obligations" and a deviation "without precedents in the history of the Stability Pact." The letter provoked another sell-off of Italian bonds and a plunge of the Milan stock market.

The next day, Moody's downgraded, as expected, the Italian debt to one notch above non-investment grade (junk). An Italian debt and banking crisis is not around the corner, as it would need four rating agencies, all issuing a "junk" rating, for the ECB to stop accepting collateral from Italian banks.

© European Union 2017

European Central Bank (ECB) president Mario Draghi.

EU

EU Commission chairman Jean-Claude Juncker.

The Hawks Are Playing with Fire

Nevertheless, the hawkish faction in the European elite is pushing a self-fulfilling prophecy as exemplified by a Reuters report of Oct. 11, which forecasts that an Italian debt crisis is inevitable, and a "Greek treatment" for Italy.

Quoting "five senior sources familiar with the ECB thinking" at the IMF summit in Bali, Reuters wrote that "the ECB's Governing Council could require that an economic program be in place in Italy before it gives its all-clear to large amounts of ECB cash being disbursed, much like it did in Greece." Reuters reminds its readers that in February 2015, the ECB first ceased accepting collateral from Greek banks, forcing them to turn to the more expensive Emergency Liquidity Assistance (ELA), and then shutting off the ELA in the summer when the Greek government refused to agree to a bailout, leaving Greece with little choice but to close the banks.

However, another faction, which according to a source includes ECB president Mario Draghi, is afraid that such tactics won't work, that Italy wouldn't back down and that would be the end of the Euro. Thus, Draghi and other EU officials recently softened their tones on Italy and invited others to do the same.

Speaking to Harley Schlanger in her Oct. 11 webcast, Schiller Institute founder Helga Zepp-LaRouche said the hawks in the EU are "playing with fire" with their confrontationist line against Italy. "The [financial] system is disintegrating, and it's just a question of time when this will happen," Mrs. LaRouche said, commenting on the IMF economic outlook report that warns of the danger of a global "depression."

In this context, Mrs. LaRouche remarked, anyone trying to put Italy up against a wall—

is playing with fire, because a banking crisis could trigger a systemic collapse. In 2008, the whole world was more or less unprepared for the crash because they were not listening to the warning my husband had already put out, very clearly, on July 25, 2007. And contrary to 2008, when everybody was unprepared, those people who are now trying to cause the Italian government to capitulate and continue with the austerity, if they push too hard, I think one should not forget that both Italian government coalition parties, the Lega and the Five Star party, have Glass-Steagall not only in their party program, but also in their coalition treaty. So, if somebody from the outside pushes them into a crash, I would not exclude the possibility, or I would actually say it's quite probable, that they would implement Glass-Steagall as a self-defense.

If the "moderate" faction in the EU prevails, there will be a formal rejection of the Italian budget proposal, but without financial warfare. This means that a "violation" procedure against Italy will be started—such procedures are routine in the EU—and sometime down the road Italy will be faced with a fine amounting to 0.2% GDP.

"It is better to pay a 0.2% fine than producing a 4% drop in GDP" as the Monti government did in 2011-2012, said Alberto Bagnai, head of the Senate Finance Commission and an ally of Savona.

If the hawkish faction prevails, get ready for Armageddon.

Plans to Cooperate with China in Africa

In related actions, the Italian government moved ahead with plans to cooperate with China for the development of Africa.

On Oct. 16, Italy's Ministry of the Environment and the Lake Chad Basin Commission signed a protocol for an Italian grant of 1.5 million Euros, to finance a feasibility study for the great Transaqua infrastructure project in Central Africa. Transaqua is a 2,400 km waterway that will refill and refresh the dying Lake Chad and, at the same time, build transport, energy and agro-industrial infrastructure that will create an economic recovery for the entire Sahel region. The Transaqua idea was developed by Italian engineers in the seventies and was in the drawer until last February when, at an international conference in Abuja, Nigeria, it was adopted by the heads of state and government of the Lake Chad basin and other African leaders.

The success of Transaqua has been the joint product of a campaign by the Schiller Institute over decades and of the relentless fight of its author, Marcello Vichi, who led the early studies for Transaqua when he was director of the Bonifica engineering firm in the seventies.

The Italian grant was announced at the Abuja conference, and the decision is now formalized. Further bureaucratic steps must follow before the study can start, but the wagon is now rolling. Romina Boldrini, CEO of Bonifica, said: "It is a historical event." Dr. Vichi added, "For the first time after many years, Africans and Europeans agree on the project." Now we must make up for the lost time."

Meanwhile, Bonifica has teamed up with the giant Chinese construction engineering company PowerChina, which is bringing its experience in building a 1,500 km canal in China and other large infrastructure. Bonifica and PowerChina have formed a strategic alliance for Transaqua and made a joint presentation at the Abuja conference.

This is a model for tripartite cooperation in Africa, which is the strategic policy promoted by the Italian government. By the end of the year, a Memo of Understanding (MOU) will be signed between Italy and China for such cooperation in the framework of the Belt and Road Initiative. Intense contacts have been going on between Italian and Chinese officials in the last months (See *EIR* Vol. 45, No. 41, Oct. 12, 2018, pp. 5-10.) As of this writing, Prime Minister Conte is meeting his Chinese colleague Li Keqiang in Brussels, while Finance Minister Giovanni Tria is receiving Tu Guangshao, Vice Chairman and President of the Chinese sovereign fund, China Investment Corporation (CIC), to work on partnering for industrial investments.

The MOU with the CIC, to be signed in 2019—in addition to the strategic one between the two governments—aims at "putting together not only capital but also know-how and analyses to promote cooperation between the two countries and begin common initiatives with direct and indirect spinoffs based on mutual dialogue."

Xinhua

Italian Prime Minister Giuseppe Conte (left) and Chinese Premier Li Keqiang, meet at the EU-ASEM leaders' summit in Brussels, Belgium on Oct. 19, 2018.

Francesco La Camera, Director General, Italian Environment Ministry (left), and Amb. Mamman Nuhu, Executive Secretary of the Lake Chad Basin Commission sign protocol for an Italian grant of 1.5 million euros to finance a feasibility study for Transaqua, on Oct. 16, 2018.

Eurogroup: A Ruthless Gang

by Leonidas Chrysanthopoulos, Ambassador *ad honorem*

Greek Ambassador Chrysanthopoulos presents below his report on the book, Adults in the Room: My Battle with Europe's Deep Establishment, *by Yanis Varoufakis, the former Finance Minister of Greece. Chrysanthopoulos was the Secretary General of the Black Sea Economic Cooperation Organization, and addressed the international Schiller Institute Conference of June 30-July 1, 2018 in Bad Soden, Germany.*

The book's author, Varoufakis, was Finance Minister of Greece from January 2015 until July 2015, in the first government of Greek Prime Minister Alexis Tsipras, who came to power on the platform of reversing the so-called European Union "bailout" of Greece during its debt crisis. That "bailout" eventually loaded Greece with a total of 340 billion euro of debt, which in reality went straight to the far more bankrupt French, German, British and other leading European banks and the International Monetary Fund, in order to "save the euro."

As Finance Minister during the first six months of the government, Varoufakis took part in the struggle between Greece and the "troika"—the European Union, European Central Bank and International Monetary Fund. His book exposes the brutal tactics used to force the eventual capitulation of the Greek government and compel it to accept yet another 80 billion euro in debt, and sign yet another so-called "memorandum" stipulating brutal austerity measures. Varoufakis was forced to resign as Finance Minister, and eventually to resign his parliamentary seat as well. He is now a professor of economics.

Chrysanthopoulos started his campaign even before the memoranda, with an interview published in December 2009 in the Greek daily newspaper Eleftherotypia *titled, "Nightmare a Fascist Europe." As a member of anti-memoranda political parties, he participated in the big demonstrations of 2011 and 2012, while at the same time writing articles and giving interviews to the foreign press. For his anti-memoranda activities, he had his title of Ambassador* ad honorem *withdrawn by presidential decree in 2013, only to be reinstated in 2016 by the Syriza government. He made demarches on human rights violations in Greece because of the austerity measures at the ministries of foreign affairs of the Benelux countries and Berlin in 2017. He submitted a complaint against Greece for human rights violations at the UN Human Rights Council in Geneva, while at the same time making speeches in various parts of Europe to publicize the deteriorating situation in Greece.*

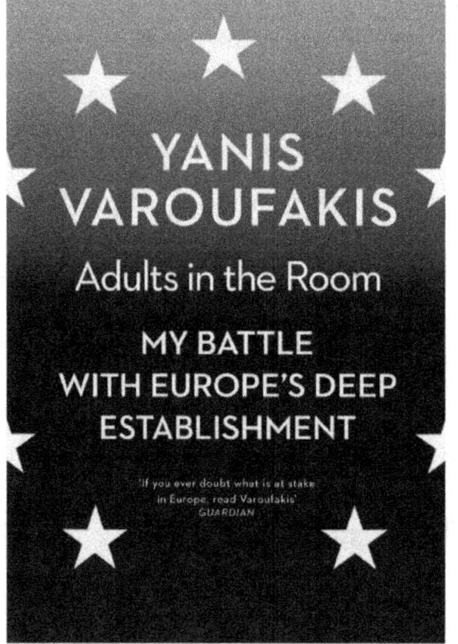

Oct. 18—On reading the last book of Y. Varoufakis, *Adults in the Room: My Battle with Europe's Deep Establishment*, the reader's interest may focus on the disgraceful methods employed by the members of the Eurozone and the EU against Greece in order to obtain its third MOU [Memorandum of Understanding]. Not that the use of such horrible methods is unknown, but now we have a first-hand account from Yanis Varoufakis, the person who negotiated with the troika during the first months of 2015.

The methods used also indicate the difficulties that the first "Anti-Memoranda" government of Greece will have to face, but by publishing them, the preparation of effective countermeasures is allowed.

The Eurogroup is an informal group of the ministers of finance of the eurozone. The EU Treaty, in its Protocol 14, Articles 1 and 2, mentions these informal meetings.

The Eurogroup used six coercive methods against Greece during the first six months of 2015 when the country was considered as an enemy state. All six will be discussed in depth below. These were 1. Extreme verbal pressure, 2. Effective blackmail, 3. Non-truths, 4. Use of Greek turncoats, 5. Pressures on third countries to abstain from financing Greece, and 6. Use of the

Yannis Varoufakis (center), Greek Minister of Finance (January-July, 2015) was given an ultimatum by Klaus Regling (right), European Stability Mechanism Managing Director, to stick with the troika's austerity program, and told by Christine Lagarde (left), IMF Managing Director, that there is no going back for Greece.

European major mass media networks for disinformation campaigns against Greece.

Extreme Verbal Pressure

The first meeting between Jeroen Dijsselbloem, the President of the Eurogroup, with Y. Varoufakis, the Greek Minister of Finance, took place on Jan. 30, 2015. After a long conversation, the Dutch Eurogroup President issued the following ultimatum: "The current program must be completed or there is nothing else."

On the margins of the first Eurogroup meeting in 2015, Christine Lagarde, the IMF's Managing Director, told Varoufakis: "These targets they insist on, can't work [referring to the troika program on Greece]. But you must understand that we have put too much on this program. We cannot go back on it. Your credibility depends on accepting and working with this program."

In March 2015, during a meeting he had with Klaus Regling, head of the European Financial Stability Facility (EFSF), Varoufakis asked him the following question: "Given that, as it seems, in a week or two we shall run out of money with which both to repay the IMF and to pay salaries and pensions, what do you advise me to do, Klaus? The choice is between defaulting on the old and frail, and defaulting to the IMF. Which is of course an unnecessary dilemma given that our central bank (ECB) owes us a similar amount," only to receive the following reply: "You must never, ever default to the IMF. Suspend all pension payments instead. This is what you must do."

What a wonderful example of the EU's social policies! Just before the Eurogroup meeting of June 27,

2015, Varoufakis met with Dijssebloem, Weiser, and Sapin, who pushed him to have the referendum cancelled. Another practice undermining the Greek positions was whenever the Greek minister took the floor during Eurogroup meetings and presented concrete compromise proposals, a silence usually followed, organized on purpose, where no other minister took the floor to comment on the proposals, thus allowing Dijssebloem to close the discussion with negative conclusions.

Effective Blackmail

Effective blackmail was in fact committed by the European Central Bank against Greece, particularly by its President, Mario Draghi. In the meeting that Varoufakis held with him on Feb. 4, 2015, and after having listened to the Greek proposals, Draghi replied by saying "And I must tell you that recent developments in Greece are putting us in a difficult position. Later today our governing board is meeting, and it is very likely that your waiver will be withdrawn." (The waiver allowed the ECB to provide Greek banks with liquidity in return for junk collateral.) The decision was taken that same evening and Greek banks were excluded from this liquidity and could now only get liquidity by the Emergency Liquidity Assistance (ELA), which was more expensive.

In its meeting of March 4, the governing board of the ECB did not revoke its previous decision in spite of the fact that the loan agreement had been extended until June 30 by the Eurogroup teleconference of Feb. 24, which was a precondition for bringing back the waiver.

When the Eurogroup meeting of June 27 rejected extending the loan agreement until July 30, so that the referendum could take place on the 28th, the governing board of the ECB revoked the ELA facility of the Central Bank of Greece in an effort to influence the outcome of the referendum.

Non-Truths

After the impasse of the Eurogroup on June 27, Dijsselbloem announced that for the first time there would be a joint communiqué without the agreement of Greece, and in the afternoon meeting, Greece would not participate. Varoufakis then asked the Secretariat: "Is the Eurogroup President at liberty to issue communiqués when there is no unanimity, and also to exclude finance ministers at will from Eurogroup meetings?"

The reply he got was the following: "Minister, the Eurogroup does not exist in law, as it is not part of any of the EU treaties. It is an informal group of the finance ministers of the eurozone member states. Thus, there are no written rules about the way it conducts its business, and therefore its president is not legally bound."

The reply was erroneous, since Protocol 10 of the EU Treaty, in its Articles 1 and 2, mentions the informal meetings of the ministers of finance of the eurozone. Had Varoufakis insisted, he could have remained in the meeting, but nothing, of course, would have changed.

On Feb. 4, in the evening, Varoufakis was scheduled to have a secret dinner with Jörg Asmussen and Jeromin Zettelmeyer, both key players in the German Social Democratic Party (SPD). As Varoufakis writes in his book:

> The purpose of the dinner was ostensibly to build bridges between the Syriza government and the section of the German government controlled by the Social Democrats.... The agreement was that I would go to the restaurant alone, incognito and by cab, and that I would not tell

CC/Jeroen Dijsselbloem

Jeroen Dijsselbloem, president of the Eurogroup, 2013-2018.

European Commission

European Central Bank President Mario Draghi.

anyone we were meeting. The implication was that it would backfire on all of us if word leaked.... Just as I was ready to leave my hotel room, I received an email from Jeromin telling me that they had changed the restaurant booking because the original restaurant was too public, confirming once more the importance of discretion.

Sometime later, Asmussen's phone rang and without saying anything on the phone, [he] gave it to Varoufakis. It was Draghi who announced to him the withdrawal of the waiver.

It seems that all Berlin knew with whom Varoufakis was having dinner that night.

Use of Greek Turncoats

Varoufakis mentions two strong supporters of the troika, the first one being the Governor of the Bank of Greece, Y. Stournaras, who from his position did everything possible to support troika policies; and the other being G. Chouliarakis, who was the troika's man in the Eurogroup and President of the Council of Economic Advisors. He represented Greece in the working group of the Eurogroup and as a close advisor to Varoufakis did everything possible to undermine his work. Today he is alternate Minister of Finance.

Pressure on Countries to Not Finance Greece

Particular and effective pressure was exercised on China. Varoufakis writes:

> The intention was to restart the formal bidding process for the Port of Piraeus under the new conditions that the Chinese had accepted, while behind the scenes the two governments agreed the Chinese loans to the Greek state.... First, Beijing would inject the remaining 1.4 billion euros of the promised 1.5 billion into our T-Bills [Treasury Bills]. Almost simultaneously, the Deputy Prime

Minister Dragasakis would make a formal trip to Beijing to strengthen relations between the two governments and informally seal the agreement. Lastly, [Prime Minister] Alexis [Tsipras] would follow up with a full state visit in April or May to make public and sign the comprehensive agreement between Athens and Beijing.

In the end, China purchased only 200 million euros of T-Bills. To quote again Varoufakis: "The next day, Alexis relayed the news from Beijing. Someone had called Beijing from Berlin with a blunt message: 'Stay out of any deals with the Greeks until we are finished with them.' " In a footnote, Varoufakis observes: "… Also lost was Beijing's readiness to help the Greek state get back on its feet (by buying government bonds) [until] when one day it regains solvency. In other words, Greece lost a strategic industrial partnership that went far beyond a port deal." This constitutes a fine example of European solidarity.

Use of Mass Media to Discredit Greek Government

The Europeans had mobilized the major mass media networks to discredit the Greek government from the outset and to perform character assassination against Varoufakis. He writes:

Of course it was the worst-kept secret in Brussels and beyond that I was to be targeted in this way. In early February 2015, around the time of my first two Eurogroup meetings, some Greek journalists were told as much by a reporter with first-hand knowledge of the campaign. One of those Greek journalists later reported the conversation: "Will Mr. Varoufakis be able to survive the pressure?" asked the reporter. "At least Mr. Tsipras still trusts him," [the Greek journalist] replied. "Then inform them in Greece, both the government and the people, that they can expect even more of these attacks," he said. Which is exactly what happened. This can be called "freedom of a manipulated mass media."

CC/Badseed

Deputy Prime Minister Yannis Dragasakis.

After such treatment, one may ask, "Why is Greece still in the eurozone and in the EU? An entire country has been destroyed in order to implement economic policies that all knew and admit would not work. Even the President of the German Bundestag, Schäuble, replying to a question of Varoufakis, if he would sign the Memorandum, were he in his place, replied in a moment of sincerity: "As a patriot, no. It is bad for your people."

Finally, in order to get rid of the bonds of the Memoranda, Greece must rely only on itself and on its people, and only when it has freed itself from these bonds, may other external factors come in to play for assistance.

Xinhua/Marios Lolos

The container ship Cosco Shipping Panama *docked at the Greek port of Piraeus, June 11, 2016.*

China 'Debt Trap' Myth Exposed

by Zaida Reyes

Zaida Reyes' article, edited here for a non-Filipino audience, was published Sept. 26 in the Daily Tribune, *newspaper in the Philippines. It is a valuable contribution to debunking the campaign by anti-China forces in the U.S. and Europe to portray China's transformational Belt and Road Initiative as an imperial policy aimed at taking over targeted nations. Readers should also look at "Why Accusations Against China for 'Debtbook Diplomacy' Are a Hoax" by Hussein Askary and Jason Ross in EIR, September 7, 2018.*

For the past few years, we have been reading incessant accusations from Western media and academic circles, then echoed in social media, about China's alleged "debt trap diplomacy."

Here in the Philippines we are also bombarded with propaganda that the Philippines-China agreements are leading the country into a debt trap with Beijing. This is a very timely subject, as the Philippines Central Bank reported on September 14 the good news that the country's foreign debt had been reduced by $997 million, to $72.2 billion.

This total foreign debt the Central Bank is reporting, is accumulated debt from the 1960s to this day, from 1961 when the U.S.-backed International Monetary Fund (IMF) compelled President Diosdado Macapagal to accept "structural adjustments," i.e., "decontrol" trade, devalue the peso and liberalize capital flows, causing the peso to slip from P2 to $1, to P3.80 to $1, and doubling the Philippines' debt to almost $400 million. Since that time the cycle of rising debt multi-

Xinhua/Liu Weibing

Philippine President Rodrigo Duterte (left) and Chinese Premier Li Keqiang (right) at Li's welcoming ceremony, Manila, Nov. 15, 2017.

plied by massive devaluation has relentlessly plagued the Philippines.

In July of this year, in a very significant statement from Finance Secretary Carlos "Sonny" Dominguez at a Senate budget hearing, the government's attitude to debt was explained: "We are not naive. We know all ODA [Official Development Assistance] projects of all countries are designed to influence. The Japanese do it, the Americans …, even Koreans…. When the Americans bombed Manila (in 1945), then gave us little money to fix it up, they extracted from us…." Clearly, the Philippines has been chained to a debt trap since the 1950s under IMF structural conditionalities that eventually led to the passing of an "automatic debt service" law in 1977.

Malacañang Palace archives

Diosdado Macapagal being sworn in as President of the Philippines, Manila, Dec. 30, 1961.

The Philippines has been chained to the IMF, World Bank and Asian Development Bank (ADB) debt trap since the 1960s, yet the so-called "Amboys" (American boys) in the country such as Magdalo's Rep. Gary Alejano, "Amboy" think tanks like the Albert del Rosario Institute and its stable of writers and talking heads such as Richard Heydarian, behave as if this fact did not exist, and instead point an accusing finger at the Duterte administration's financial dealings with China, constituting such a miniscule amount today, as the "debt trap" problem.[1]

Win-Win with China

On the sidelines of a Senate Finance Committee hearing August 27, Alan Peter Cayetano, Secretary of Foreign Affairs, told reporters the startling fact that loans from China today constitute only no more than one percent of foreign debt, that it could not possibly pose any danger of becoming a "debt trap." In all likelihood, there will never be a China trap

U.S. Army photo showing destruction of the Walled City district of Old Manila in May, 1945, after the Battle of Manila.

---

1. Editor's note: Rep. Gary Alejano was part of two military insurrections against the Philippine government, in 2003 and 2007, spent four years in prison, but was pardoned and then elected to Congress. He led an impeachment effort against President Duterte in 2017. Albert del Rosario was Ambassador to the U.S., then Foreign Minister under former President Noynoy Aquino. He was a close advisor to President Cory Aquino, who was placed in office by the George Shultz-orchestrated coup against nationalist President Ferdinand Marcos in 1986. Richard Heydarian, a fellow at the Albert del Rosario Institute, is a regular contributor to CSIS and CFR forums and publications.

as the Filipino people have become so alert to that very bitter experience with the IMF, WB and ADB that everyone in this country is looking under every rug to detect any such danger.

Another significant fact is that much of China's financial commitment so far has come in the form of grants, for the two bridges over Pasig [the river running through Manila], the multimillion-peso drug rehab centers in Mindanao, and assistance programs such as that for the Hybrid Rice program at the Central Luzon State University, as well as financial assistance to the victims of past calamities and major crises like the Marawi siege [a five-month battle in 2017 to free a major city in Mindanao seized by terrorists]. All loan packages for components of President Duterte's infrastructure program, known as "Build, Build, Build," are productive projects that ensure earnings to pay back such loans.

Upcoming Mega-Projects

The real big-ticket financing will be signed this coming November during the planned state visit of China's President Xi Jinping to the Philippines. One of these major projects is the $3.5 billion loan agreement for the construction of the Philippines' legendary Bicol Express [connecting Manila with the Bicol Peninsula in the southeast of the main island of Luzon], or the $3.2 billion, 600 km Manila-

Xinhua/Dong Chengwen

Administrator Ricardo Visaya speaks at the June 13, 2018 groundbreaking of President Duterte's flagship infrastructure project, financed and built by China.

Matnog rail line [on the southern tip of the Bicol Peninsula]. This project constitutes about 14 percent of the $24 billion investment deals agreed between Presidents Xi Jinping and President Rodrigo R. Duterte during the historic October 2016 visit of the latter to China—which is an amazingly fast pace of development.

Yet, even before this mega government-to-government project is signed, privately led Chinese investments have already been arriving by the droves. Prof. Alvin Camba, a Filipino doctoral candidate at Johns Hopkins University, wrote this in the July 19 issue of *The Diplomat*:

A year and a half later (after President Duterte's visit to China in 2016), newspapers have argued that the predicted boom has failed to materialize. (But) according to actualized FDI data of the Central Bank of the Philippines, China and Hong Kong's FDI inflows (which should be counted as one) had already reached $1.06 billion by March 2018 (surpassing) the entirety of Chinese and Hong Kong investments received under former President Gloria Arroyo ($828 million) and already reached five-sixths of the $1.2 billion under former president Benigno Aquino's term.

Xinhua/Rouelle Umali

Philippine President Rodrigo Duterte (center) breaks ground for two China-funded bridges in Manila, July 17, 2018.

Mid-year in 2019, Package Two, consisting of rails and bridges in the Visayan island and Mindanao, water supply and flood control projects in Metro Manila and Luzon, industrial parks from North to South of the country, and a host of other projects worth billions more will be signed. The Philippines-China financial and infrastructure deals, with rates at or just above 2 percent interest, are actually financial assistance packages to help develop Third World economies to become mature economies, able to both supply and consume goods and services in the regional and global market.

So let's get it straight: The "debt trap" has been the legacy of the Western Powers working through their multilateral financial institutions—the IMF, World Bank and the Japanese-led ADB. This debt trap scheme has been recorded in books of John Perkins, particularly his account of his personal experience as a "loan consultant" of the Western financial institutions assigned to developing countries. Perkins' 2004 book, *Confessions of an Economic Hitman*, recounts the methods by which Third World country leaders are entrapped, and how the Western Powers arranged to get rid of any uncooperative leaders.

January 15, 2001

The New Bretton Woods System: Framework for a New, Just World Economic Order

by Lyndon H. LaRouche, Jr.[1]

Keynote to a Jan. 14-17, 2001 conference in Khartoum, organized jointly by the Center for Strategic Studies and the Ministry of Culture and Information of Sudan, and EIR *and the Schiller Institute.*

The opening days of the year 2001, have unleashed what will quickly prove to be the worst, already long-overdue, global financial collapse in the recent centuries of history of today's globally extended form of modern European civilization. Unless certain corrective actions are taken soon, by some concert among a significant number of governments, this will quickly become, in a matter of months, not only the worst economic depression in recent world history, but also what is known in the economics literature as a global economic-breakdown crisis.

Although the presently accelerating global financial collapse, is far worse than that of the 1929-1933 interval, the lessons of the U.S. economic recovery, under the leadership of President Franklin Roosevelt, provide us today an historical precedent, on which the world as a whole could rely with confidence, for overcoming that far more severe economic crisis being unleashed at the present moment. Important historical lessons are also to be learned from the successful post-war recovery of both the U.S.A. and western Europe, during the first two decades following the close of the great war of 1939-1945.

We must also learn from what the U.S.A. and Europe failed to do, which would have been done, had President Roosevelt not died prematurely. As Roosevelt made clear, repeatedly, to Britain's Prime Minister Winston Churchill, as in the 1942 meeting at Casablanca, it had been the President's intention, once the war had ended, to use the great power of the U.S.A. to force the immediate dissolution of the Portuguese, Dutch, British, and French colonial systems, and to unleash programs for large-scale infrastructure development and technological improvements of the productive powers of labor among the peoples of the nations liberated from imperial domination.

Thus, although good things were done by the U.S.A. in rebuilding the war-shattered economies of western Europe and of Japan, around the ideas of such figures as France's Jean Monnet and the Schuman plan, Roosevelt's body was scarcely cold, before his successors acted, in concert with the British monarchy, to reimpose, by military force, old imperial and colonial tyrannies over the former Portuguese, Dutch, British, and French colonies and semi-colonies.

These assorted experiences from the 1929-1965 period, have the most vital importance for policy-makers throughout the world today. These lessons from history, show us what past models we must copy, and which we must avoid, in acting now to establish the reorganized world monetary system needed to cope with the disastrous economic effects of the present global financial collapse, disastrous effects,

---

1. Economist Lyndon H. LaRouche, Jr. is currently a candidate for the Year 2004 U.S. Presidential nomination.

which will be felt by all nations of the world, without exception.

We must not make the probably fatal mistake, of rejecting those models as precedents for today's actions, simply because they are specific to that period of history, or because of acquired hostility to the image of the United States. The survival of civilization in every part of the world today, depends upon reaching prompt and far-reaching agreements on what present opinion will regard as revolutionary changes in international monetary and related institutions. No such agreement were possible, if our reforms did not carry the authority of clear and successful precedents formerly applied to circumstances similar, on many points, to the crisis in full swing today.

For such reasons, any proposed reforms for today, would fail for political reasons, unless the measures to be taken now were clearly identified as modelled upon the successful features of the revolutionary changes made then.

What Must Be Done

I now summarize, first, the kinds of measures which must be instituted very soon, to bring the presently global financial collapse under control, and, then, secondly, indicate the problems which could not be overcome without exactly those types of emergency measures of international monetary reform. Then, thirdly, finally, I shall summarize certain crucial features of the currently unfolding strategic situation against that economic backdrop.

To bring about both a halt to the presently ongoing world-wide collapse, and to launch a recovery, we must take three classes of essential measures.

First, we must restore the characteristics of the old Bretton Woods system of the immediate post-war decades. That means, a system of fixed-exchange rates, capital controls, currency controls, and financial controls, and global growth fostered by the same methods employed through institutions such as Germany's Kreditanstalt für Wiederaufbau, to promote large-scale development of basic economic infrastructure, and to use the market potential generated by that infrastructural development, as the base for creating a still-larger rate of growth in development of agriculture and industry.

Second, we must do as President Roosevelt had intended: all sovereign nations must be, on principle, full partners in the new international monetary system. This is the fundamental difference between the old Bretton Woods system, and what must happen now. We cannot have a system which is going to work, which does not treat the majority of the human race as full partners in the system. Otherwise, it won't work.

Third, we must rely chiefly on credit created by the authority of perfectly sovereign nation-state governments, to generate the medium- to long-term, domestic and international trade agreements on which the economic recovery and expansion will be centered.

Now, let me interpolate, because there is a lot of information coming out of Europe, and especially the United States, to the contrary. First of all, *this crash is happening now.* It is not a *recession,* it is not a *soft landing;* it is a full-scale collapse of the entire system. The entire world financial and monetary system is about to disintegrate. Nothing can keep this system alive in the coming period. Any information to the contrary is false. And therefore, the only thing that is inevitable about the situation, is the fact that the system is about to collapse. What happens when the system collapses, is where the options lie. In a situation in which none of the existing, privately controlled central banking systems and international institutions are capable of generating credit, in any significant amounts, you must tear down and replace the present system of credit generation. And there's only one way you can do it, and that is by using the power of sovereign governments, to assert their sovereign commitment, for credit for largely long-term trade agreements. That is, the state agrees to enter into a partnership with another state, or group of states, for long-term trade, such as the exchange of goods over a longer period of time, against capital infusions. It's the only way it can be done. There is no other way that it will work; no other possibilities exist, despite all the talk about free trade and globalization. None of those things can possibly work. They're *doomed.* They're popular, but they're doomed.

Such measures as I propose will be made feasible, through actions taken either by sovereign governments or agencies of cooperation among such governments, which put the existing, generally bankrupt central banking systems of the world through the absolutely unavoidable process of medium- to long-term reorganization in bankruptcy.

Unless each and all of such measures are taken, and that soon, by a significant number of governments, the present economic situation will be more or less a hope-

The first step into Hell: President Nixon's shift toward the "Southern Strategy," which led to the collapse of the Bretton Woods agreements in August 1971. Here: Henry Kissinger with the President, 1971.

Step 2: Zbigniew Brzezinski's choice for President, Jimmy Carter, wreaks havoc with the U.S. economy. Here, Carter with members of his Cabinet, including Brzezinski (behind Carter, to his left).

less one, world-wide, and will continue so for a generation or more to come.

It is only the precedents to which I referred, from the experience of the 1929-1965 interval, which provide the basis for agreement on action among at least a significant number of nations today. Therefore my leading concern, in my various activities in many parts of the world, has been to place in the hands of the nations and their leaders the knowledge and confidence which are needed to strengthen their will to act in a timely fashion in support of those lessons from the recent past of world history.

How the U.S. Took Five Steps into Hell

The present world financial collapse, is chiefly an outgrowth of the radiated, world-wide impact of a process of post-1965 ruin of a U.S. economy which had been, with all its faults, the most successful model the world had known, prior to that time. There are five leading developments which have, in succession, brought about this self-destruction within the U.S.A. itself.

The most dramatic current expression of this thirty-five-year-long moral and economic decline inside the U.S. itself, is the currently accelerating collapse of the role of the U.S. economy as the "importer of last resort." This presently ongoing turn, means a collapse of that part of the market upon which most among the world's nations had each recently come to depend for a critical margin of its own domestic economic life.

Those five steps downward, and their bearing on the presently accelerating collapse of the U.S. as an import market, are summarily, as follows.

This first step began during the 1966-1968 campaign of former Vice-President Richard Nixon for the 1968 Republican Presidential nomination. During that 1966-68 campaign, Nixon and his circles made a coalition with those sections of the U.S. Democratic Party base which harbored the pro-racist legacy of that Confederacy which President Abraham Lincoln had defeated in the great Civil War of 1861-65. This pro-racist, Nixon-led turn, was known then and later, as the so-called Southern Strategy, a Southern Strategy, sometimes also called "The Third Way," which is still the

Step 3: The Reagan-Bush Administration ushers in the era of junk bonds and financial derivatives speculation.

Step 4: Margaret Thatcher and George Bush, along with France's François Mitterrand, set into motion the policy known as "globalization," to destroy the world's nation-states.

leading political force inside the U.S. today.

In addition to being a revival of pro-racist sentiments and policies inside the U.S. political party-system, there were certain related shifts in economic policy, away from the so-called Yankee traditions of technological progress in agriculture and industry, large-scale infrastructure improvements, and improvements of the general welfare of the population as a whole. Thus, the pro-racist trend represented by Nixon's Southern Strategy, was accompanied by an increasingly radical "free trade" ideology.

This combination in U.S. domestic and foreign policy under Nixon and Henry A. Kissinger, led into the collapse of the Bretton Woods agreements in August 1971. The effects of that, combined with Kissinger's orchestration of such developments as the 1973 Middle East war, unleashed a terrible ruin within the U.S. economy.

The second, even worse blow to the economy, was brought about through Zbigniew Brzezinski's choice for President, the pro-Southern Strategy Jimmy Carter. The rampage of deregulation and related destructive measures under Carter, did far more ruin to the U.S.

economy than has occurred under any other U.S. President since Nixon's election in 1968. The worst of these measures introduced under Carter, were the work of Carter's appointment of Paul Volcker as Chairman of the U.S. Federal Reserve System. Volcker's policies, as continued under his designated successor, Alan Greenspan, have continued and aggravated that ruin, up to the present day.

The third blow came beginning 1982, under President Ronald Reagan and Vice-President George Bush. Terribly destructive legislation that year, such as Garn-St Germain and Kemp-Roth, arranged for financial speculators' picking of the bones of the banking and other institutions which Carter's policies had ruined. This was the era of the junk bond, and the beginning of what became the vast financial-derivatives bubble which is exploding the financial system of the world today.

The fourth blow, came in the concerted actions of Britain's Prime Minister Margaret Thatcher, France's President François Mitterrand, and U.S. President George Bush, in the handling of the disintegration of the Soviet system. Mrs. Thatcher, who was obsessed with the desire to destroy the economy of Germany, allied with Mrs. Thatcher's Germany-hating asset Mitterrand, and Bush, to reduce all of continental Europe from status of ally, to Anglo-American lackey, systematically destroying the real economy of nations throughout continental Europe, including the former Soviet Union. What was thus set into motion, during 1989-1992, was the emergence of a new world empire, an Anglo-American imperium, called "globalization." This imperial monster, conceived in imitation of the ancient Roman empire, set itself to the task of uprooting, world-wide, not only the political and financial institutions of the sovereign nation-state, but also the ability of national economies to produce even their most essential margins of needs within their own borders.

In this fourth step, even the sovereignty of the United States itself has been systematically destroyed, a virtual act of treason, in favor of an opposing power, world government, which aimed at becoming an imperial form of English-speaking world-wide rule.

The fifth blow, was the fruit of great financial fraud played on the world as a whole. This fraud, known as "Y2K," was perpetrated through an organized panic, known as the fear that the advent of January 1, 2000, would cause a chain-reaction financial collapse.

It was said that this collapse would be caused by widespread dependency of governments and businesses upon computer systems which had based their programs on a two-final-digit code for date, would not do their proper work when confronted with a two-final-digit code "00." During the several years preceding 2000, a vast amount of financial capital was created, to flow into certain measures which might, hopefully, prevent such a Year 2000 crisis. This gigantic swindle was the celebrated cult of "Y2K."

Under the influence of this panic, vast amounts of financial capital were created, to be poured into not only investments in reprogramming computers, but purchasing new computer systems better suited to overcoming the "Y2K" threat. On top of these amounts, a vast financial reserve was created and set aside for the alleged purpose of readiness to cope with the allegedly inevitable threat of a January 1, 2000 "Y2K" collapse of almost everything!

Call it the "Y2K financial bubble." What actually happened, was that, given the global financial collapse already impending for the mid-1990s, Federal Reserve

Step 5: Federal Reserve Chairman Alan Greenspan perpetrates the fraud known as "Y2K," pumping vast amounts of money into the financial system, in a desperate effort to maintain the speculative bubble.

Chairman Alan Greenspan and others created a vast diversionary financial scheme, whose relatively short-lived result was the gigantic public-relations hoax called "new economy."

During the run-up, from the mid-1990s to January 1, 2000, the development of the Internet was used to create a vast diversion, which absorbed gigantic amounts of credit pumped into the financial markets, notably the markets for so-called "information technology" and its by-products. The computer industry, the software industry, and the marketing schemes associated with promotion of the Internet for such purposes, were hyper-inflated to impossible financial altitudes. The Eighteenth-Century speculator, John Law, would have been amazed that a modern people could be so credulous as the now-bankrupt financial titans of the "new economy" have been.

In March 2000, there were signs that the "new economy" bubble was ripe for inevitable popping. To delay that collapse, oceanic floods of credit, such as that organized by the notorious "plunge protection committees," moved to prop up an intrinsically bankrupt NASDAQ sector, and also to attempt to manage the delicate relations of all of this to the U.S. banking sector. However, like all financial bubbles, this one was kept alive a bit longer, at a terrible price to the real economy on whose back it sat as a parasite.

During all of that, the process of globalization was building the preconditions for what is now becoming clearly a collapse of the world's principal export market, the U.S. role as "the importer of last resort."

Beginning about March 2000, the first clear signs of the threatened collapse in the illusory "new economy" financial bubble, were reflected in financial markets. This collapse of that bubble reflected the combined effects of other forms of long-term degeneration in the U.S. and world economy.

To understand how the presently accelerating collapse of the U.S. as an import market, affects the world economy at large, some of these other leading factors must be taken into account.

The World Economy Is Now Collapsing

Apparently, few professionals from around the world ever gave the attention they should have given, to a series of published reports, issued by the New York Council on Foreign Relations as the long-range strategic plan, written and published beginning 1975-76, intended to be set into motion by Zbigniew Brzezinski's puppet, U.S. President Jimmy Carter. This "Project 1980s" series, later published in full by McGraw-Hill, outlined what has become, since that time, the philosophy underlying virtually every critical measure in economic and social policy of the U.S. government, from the time of Carter's inauguration, on.

Among the leading features of this operational strategic plan was an explicit proposal for causing "a controlled disintegration of the economy." This policy, introduced by that name, was put fully into operation by President Carter's Fall 1979 appointment of Paul Volcker as Chairman of the U.S. Federal Reserve System. This policy, so specified, in both name and deed, by Volcker, has been the continuing kernel of the monetary and economic policy of the U.S. Federal Reserve System, under Volcker and his only successor, Alan Greenspan, ever since.

That policy has worked just as it was explicitly designed to work. This policy has brought about a process of controlled disintegration of the collective economy of virtually the entire world. When we have felt more fully, very soon, the impact of the presently ongoing collapse of the U.S. economy as the world's importer of last resort, China, too, with its dependency upon for-eign investments in its cheap-labor-produced export categories, will be among the nations struck with the challenge represented by the fully destructive force of the Volcker-Greenspan policy of controlled disintegration.

There can be no competent assessment of any among the leading features of international financial, monetary, and economic developments over the course of the recent thirty-five years, without studying those developments in the light of the impact of the five steps of change in U.S. policy I have just identified. Any different view of the matter must be considered as incompetent, by virtue of the principle of fallacy of composition of the evidence.

As any among us might read the official statements of most of the leading governments and leading economists of those nations and of the IMF and World Bank, and most of the world's leading press, until recent weeks, we have the following picture of the incompetence of those economists. Virtually every one of what the leading international press has called "mainstream" economists, the economists on which most governments have credulously relied, are now exposed, with rare exceptions, as having issued a totally incompetent analysis and forecast of recent and present trends in the economy of the world as a whole.

Overall, the establishment of the so-called "floating-exchange-rate monetary system," as set into motion by U.S. President Nixon during August 1971, has been a world-wide catastrophe, especially in its effects upon the foreign-debt balances and internal economies of so-called developing nations. However, the worst structural damage to the world economy occurred under President Carter, not Nixon. The key is the doctrine of "controlled disintegration" unleashed upon the world by that Carter Administration. The form of the presently ongoing collapse of the role of the U.S. as importer of last resort, is chiefly the result of those specific actions set into motion under Brzezinski's puppet-President Carter.

Concentrate on the transformation of the U.S., from its pre-1977 post-war role as, in partnership with western Europe and Japan, as the world's leading exporter of technology, to the ruined U.S. economy's pitiable present economic condition as importer of last resort for the world at large.

Since the beginning of the modern form of nation-state, during Europe's Fifteenth Century, the growth of the population, life-expectancy, and prosperity of the world, has been chiefly the effect of two factors spreading world-wide from that birth of the nation-state.

First, was the establishing of the sovereign nation-state on the basis of the principle that government has no morally legitimate authority to rule, except as it is efficiently dedicated to promotion of what is called the general welfare, or common good, of the population and its posterity as a whole.

Second, the role of a national commitment to scientific and technological progress, as the driving-force for improvements in both the productivity and general welfare of the nation.

Contrary to much popularized mythology, the generator of great technological progress has not been the giant stockholders' corporation, but rather those technologically energetic smaller enterprises, such as machine-tool enterprises, which reflect a disposition for risk-taking in the areas of development of scientific and technological progress. These are the usually smaller, or medium-sized enterprises, usually the creation of private entrepreneurs, not stock markets. The ability of the large manufacturing corporation to generate production of improved products, has depended chiefly on the role of the medium-sized enterprises which have shown great flexibility and powers of rapid innovation, as suppliers to the giant industrial enterprises.

Carter's measures struck directly against two crucial areas of any successful modern economy.

First, was the rolling back of maintenance and development of basic economic infrastructure. In a modern, healthy agro-industrial economy, these expenditures, largely through government-regulated categories of investment, have amounted to about one-third, or even sometimes more, of the total value of physical output of the national economy as a whole. This was approximately the formula followed by the Franklin Roosevelt Administration, in bringing about the great, accelerating U.S. economic recovery of the 1933-1945 interval.

Second, Carter struck down both investment and regulation of vital areas of infrastructure, but also three other Achilles'-heel sectors of the U.S. economy: the independent, high-technology family farm, the small entrepreneurial business sector, and the credit institutions upon which agriculture and small closely held industries depended for their continued existence. The

destruction of the smaller entrepreneurial sectors of agriculture and industry under Carter, was ferocious, sudden, and never repaired to the present day. The most concentrated destruction of the U.S. economy on these accounts, of both basic economic infrastructure and technologically progressive agro-industrial entrepreneurial activity, struck with the greatest force under the initial, 1979-1982, period of Volcker's reign as Federal Reserve Chairman.

Over the course of the 1980s, and especially since the 1989-91 collapse of the Soviet system, the U.S. sources of technology shifted, from earlier reliance on U.S. entrepreneurial and scientific activity, to imports from cheaper-labor areas of the world. As a result of this trend, the U.S. of the past decade, has lost its quality as a "full set" economy, to become dependent for its very physical existence on growing rations of cheap imports, including machine-tool imports, from less economically fortunate regions of the world. Since 1989-1990, the same trend has taken over, with great and accelerating force in Germany and other parts of Europe.

By late in the year 2000, the U.S. dependency on imports had reached levels which were reflected in part by an estimated annual rate of U.S. current-account deficit in the order of about $600 billions a year. If we consider weighting factors, some of them hidden under the cloak of financial sleight-of-hand, a major collapse of the U.S. as an importer of last resort for the world market is now erupting. The effects on the nations of the world, especially the areas which have been used as sources of cheap-labor exports to the U.S.A., will be massive. The impact on Mexico will be among the worst cases, relatively speaking; but the impact upon all of the economies of East, Southeast, and East Asia, to say nothing of Africa, will be among the most important strategic effects.

The Timing of This Collapse

To understand why the presently ongoing global financial collapse was inevitable during approximately this time, one must compare the way in which the effects of the "Y2K" bubble echoed the 1923 eruption of hyperinflation in Weimar Germany.

Weimar Germany's inflationary printing-press money-issues had been used to roll over the World War I allies' war-reparations and other debts imposed on defeated Germany. When the point was reached,

The Collapse Reaches a Critical Point of Instability

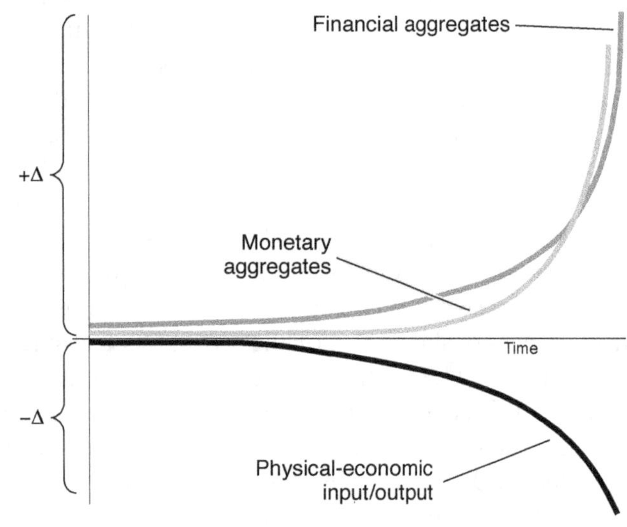

during early Summer 1923, that this inflationary print-ing-press tactic was costing more, in terms of inflation-ary effects, than the total debt being rolled over by such methods, the inflation in money-printing exploded into a spiral of commodity-price hyperinflation.

During the course of early 2000, an analogous effect came to the surface from inside the methods of inflationary pump-priming used, since 1998, by what came to be known as the U.S. "plunge protection com-mittee" of Fed Chairman Alan Greenspan, and Robert Rubin subordinate and successor Treasury Secretary Larry Summers, et al. During early months of the Y2000 U.S. Presidential primary-election campaigns, it became evident that the rate of financial pump-prim-ing required was becoming significantly greater than the amount of debt being rolled over in this way. A sit-uation of potential commodity-price inflation, analo-gous to that of 1923 Weimar Germany, had developed. [See **Figure 1.**]

The choice between commodity-price hyperinfla-tion and collapse of the role of the U.S. as importer of last resort, was shown clearly by hyperinflationary trends in energy prices, in real estate occupancy prices, and in many categories of manufacturers' supplies. At that point, the sole mission of continued "plunge pro-tection committee" and related efforts, was to postpone the financial collapse until after the Nov. 7 U.S. Presi-dential election. The crisis in energy policy now erupt-ing in the U.S. state of California, typifies the condi-tions which made the present stage of the U.S. crisis inevitable for about this time.

This collapse of the U.S. bubble has the following notable global impact on the U.S.A.'s former role as importer of last resort.

As long as the U.S. financial market was apparently the market of the highest yield on relatively short-term flows of financial capital, the U.S. financial bubble was able to aid the U.S. in forcing multi-trillions-dollar annual rates of inflow of financial capital from around the world, notably including the Euro- and Yen-carry-trade areas. The speculative financial gains on U.S. fi-nancial markets were thus able to offset, not only the massive and upward-spiralling U.S. current account deficit, but to maintain the U.S. in the role of importer of last resort for the world at large.

Now, that role has ended. The blow-back against those nations which have depended on the U.S. market, will be tremendous. The effect on Mexico will be cata-strophic. Similar trends will be experienced throughout East and other parts of the Asian littoral. For Africa, the combined direct and indirect effects will be catastrophe piled upon calamity.

The Strategic Implications

At this time, there is world-wide interest in discov-ering what might be the actual strategic outlook of the incoming U.S. Administration. As to what representa-tives of that Administration are saying on that subject, what is widely reported is in fact a mixture of willful deception by such sources, and also an even larger dose of self-deception by the Administration itself. The U.S. and its political institutions, are presently in the grip of a global catastrophe far beyond what the incoming Ad-ministration is willing to contemplate. It is fairly said, that the incoming Administration is a spectacle of Clas-sical tragedy on an epochal scale.

To be as brief as possible, the following are the lead-ing considerations to be borne in mind.

In the Biblical book of Jonah, there is an account of Jonah's reluctant mission to deliver a message to the people of the city of Nineveh. God offered Nineveh a choice, to save itself, or be destroyed. Think of my role as that of a not-reluctant Jonah, delivering a warning to my own government. It is impossible to predict what U.S. policy will be, even in the short term. The incoming Administration does not know what its actual policy will become during the course of the crisis-wracked weeks ahead. The U.S. might doom itself, as Nineveh did by rejecting Jonah's warning, or, it might accept the warning, and thus, as Jonah's message promised, survive.

No one alive today, including the new U.S. Administration, could predict anything but the general nature of the choices being presented, and the general nature of the consequences of selecting either of those sets of choices. The choice is one that that Administration will consider awful.

If the new Administration attempts to limit its policy-choices to the set of commitments which it and its leading advisors have maintained up to this point, the U.S.A. as we have known it, is presently doomed. It could survive, and that rather well, only by abandoning what it has adopted as its so-called political principles up to this time. Thus, as is the case in every great Classical tragedy, the doom of a regime, a nation, is brought about because the nation prefers to cling to its acquired habits, rather than choose the contrary pathway of reason.

That choice can be fairly described as an elementary one.

Since the crisis is the outcome of a series of closely related policy-changes instituted over the recent thirty-five years, the crisis must be recognized as one which could be terminated only by abandoning and reversing those policy-changes. In effect, that would mean returning to the kinds of policy-making standards which were in force under President Kennedy and under the pre-1966 Presidency of Lyndon Johnson. The difficulty inhering in that kind of problem, is that the relevant political and other institutions have been radically transformed in character since the successful drive of Richard Nixon to secure election as President.

Changes of that deep-going kind usually occur only as what are perceived to be actual, or virtual political revolutions. Moreover, such revolutions are most unlikely, except under conditions of great shock to the existing system. Thus, the question is twofold. First, whether the shock now in the process of being experienced, would be sufficiently strong to make such a radical change in policy-matrix possible at this time? Second, whether the needed new policies have become sufficiently widespread knowledge, and have sufficient support from among at least some influential circles and institutions, to make the required changes a clearly visible political alternative?

Certainly, on the first account, the shock in the process of being experienced, is more or less as strong and profound as any experienced in recent history. On the second, there are reasons for doubt. Although my own proposals are widely known, and do have increasing support from important circles around the world, as well as in the United States, there is still room for doubt that my initiatives could be successful. If not, then, the U.S.A. as we have known it heretofore, is assuredly doomed during the near term. Worse, unless some powerful combination of states can act in concert, in the directions I have indicated as necessary, the prospect for the world as a whole, is little better than that for my country itself.

I have given you a grim picture, but, the only accurate and honest one possible. We have our implied options, and we must proceed with the intent for success, whatever we must face in that effort to overcome the obstacles before us. True solutions will be found, only when realistic assessment of challenges before us, is accepted.

Kesha Rogers: Independent 'Classical' Candidate for Congress from Texas' 9th C.D.

Oct. 23—In an interview today, less than two weeks before the November 6 Midterm elections, independent candidate Kesha Rogers stressed that her campaign is finding an absolute thirst for big ideas and the types of crash-program problem solving that is characteristic of the space program. Rogers, who is spearheading the LaRouche PAC's Campaign to Secure the Future's intervention into the Midterms, is running as an independent in Texas' 9th C.D. against incumbent Democrat Al Green.

Green positioned himself to lead the insane impeachment drive for the Democrats against Donald Trump in grandstanding Congressional speeches in 2017 and early 2018. In those speeches, Green proclaimed, contrary to the explicit words of the Constitution, that impeachment was a matter of partisan whim, that the Constitution did not require that the President commit any crime to be impeached. As a result, Green received a flood of donations from Democratic organizations nationally, while doing virtually nothing for his district, which is one of the poorest districts in Texas.

The 9th C.D. was gerrymandered by former House Speaker Tom Delay to dump significant minority populations into one district, in order to protect Republican majorities in other districts in the Houston metropolitan area. Some say the district was even deliberately created for Al Green in 2004, in order to specifically ensure his Democratic seat in Congress.

"I chose this District as a challenge," Rogers said, "because even in its creation it exemplifies exactly the

Kesha Rogers, Independent, CD 9, calls out Greedy Al Green

But Greedy Al just cuts and runs. He really thinks you can't see who he is.

Cartoons lampooning Rogers' opponent, Democrat incumbent Greedy Al Green, who has introduced legislation to impeach President Trump. Multi-millionaire Green presides over one of the poorest districts in Texas.

type of partisan and identity politics which have failed us and turned statecraft into a small-minded spectator sport, resulting in whole sections of our population being stuck in place, going nowhere, or far worse. Al Green presides over this district like an entitled slum lord, doling out small favors and small programs to make abject poverty somehow more comfortable.

"By contrast, I embrace the ideas of Martin Luther King, Bobby Kennedy, and Lyndon LaRouche: Poverty is not a natural human condition. It is evil. It is something to be completely broken and conquered.

"The first pledge of LaRouche PAC's Campaign to Secure the Future is to end the British-inspired coup against Donald Trump and the threat of impeachment. That will continue if the Democrats have a resounding victory in House races. If it continues, then we face a period of absolute chaos right at a time when the financial system, built on a new monstrous monetary bubble, faces a new and more threatening collapse than that we suffered in 2008.

"All along, the impeachment drive against Trump has been for one purpose: Get him to give up his big ideas about supporting Glass-Steagall and the American System of political economy, and his intent to have sane relationships with Russia and China. Get him to depend so much on the extant corrupt party machinery that either he loses popular support and can be impeached or, in order to pragmatically survive politically, he returns to the failed programs of George Bush and Barack Obama, which have practically destroyed this nation.

"At the Trump-Ted Cruz rally last night, we had a big response to LaRouche PAC's leaflet, 'The 2018 Midterms Are Humanity's Big Chance: Don't Blow It on a Bunch of Crazies Paid for by George Soros.' People were both surprised and intrigued to think about the actual stakes here, including war and peace, rather than remaining in the fox hole thinking which they are fed by the media every day."

The leaflet features a cartoon contrasting Rogers' bold future vision for humanity with Al Green's singular devotion to Donald Trump's impeachment.

Radio, Classical Music & Rogers' Program

On Oct. 22, President Trump held a huge rally in Houston with 32,000 people, close to 100,000 people had tried to attend. The Rogers campaign was there in force, emphasizing that support for the President had to now bear fruit in the fulfillment of his campaign promises concerning Glass-Steagall banking separation, and the American system of political economy which, by its nature, could generate massive amounts of credit for

EIRNS/Brian Barajas
Rogers campaign banner welcoming President Trump to Houston, Oct. 22, 2018.

Kesha Rogers (right) reaches out to Trump supporters at the Houston Trump rally.

EIRNS/Gabriela Carr

renewing and modernizing major national economic infrastructure.

These promises not only need to be implemented, but expanded to fulfill the other conditions for economic prosperity specified in Lyndon LaRouche's Four Laws for Economic Recovery. "With credit directed toward projects with a mandate to increase the productive powers of labor and living standards, we now need a crash program for fusion power development which can transform raw materials into new resources and power space exploration. Space exploration, in turn, is the next big human frontier, and a crash program for Moon-Mars exploration presents an opportunity for collaboration among the United States, Russia, China, and India to solve basic scientific problems for all of mankind, while providing the foundation for a durable world peace," Rogers said.

The Rogers campaign is now running radio ads on Houston's major gospel station and will expand this week to running an ad campaign on the major Spanish station. These ads contrast Al Green's Johnny-One-

Note cash plea about impeachment with Kesha Rogers' bold vision for the future of the district; at the same time the ads hit pressing economics concerns highlighted by emphasis on restoring Glass-Steagall; the need for massive infrastructure building, including long-delayed flood control systems for Houston in the wake of Hurricane Harvey; solving the immigration crisis by ending free trade and developing Mexico and Central America; and returning NASA to a greatly expanded and active manned space exploration mission. More ads and videos are being produced this week.

Kesha Rogers energizes constituents at Trump's Houston Rally, Oct. 22, 2018.

A major theme of Rogers' campaign has been the need for a return to a classical curriculum and classical education. Her central and repeated idea is that every child's genius is fostered and developed under such a program. She cites an example of such genius, the case of Katherine Johnson, who not only calculated how John Glenn could orbit the Earth and return to earth safely, how Apollo astronauts could return to their capsule from the Moon, but who also broke down every racial barrier with her passionate determination and genius.

On Oct. 25, the Rogers campaign is holding an event to debunk the recent climate change report by the Intergovernmental Panel on Climate Change (IPCC), which Rogers' called an "undisguised attempt to impose population control, zero growth, and genocide on large parts of this planet." On Oct. 27, her campaign is sponsoring a classical music concert called, "The Sweet Power of Music to Unify and Uplift the Nation."

www.ingramcontent.com/pod-product-compliance
Lightning Source LLC
Chambersburg PA
CBHW081600270726
48657CB00029B/3444